Walks in Mysterious Somerset

Laurence Main

Published by Sigma Leisure – an imprint of Sigma Press, 1 South Oak Lane, Wilmslow, Cheshire SK9 6AR, England.

British Library Cataloguing in Publication Data
A CIP record for this book is available from the British Library.

ISBN: 1-85058-664-0

Typesetting and Design by: Sigma Press, Wilmslow, Cheshire.

Cover photograph: The Holy Thorn on Wearyall Hill with Glastonbury Tor in the background *(Laurence Main)*

Photographs: Laurence Main

Maps: Alan Bradley

Printed by: MFP Design and Print

Disclaimer: the information in this book is given in good faith and is believed to be correct at the time of publication. No responsibility is accepted by either the author or publisher for errors or omissions, or for any loss or injury howsoever caused. Only you can judge your own fitness, competence and experience.

'Here are Mysteries Indeed'

~ a Foreword by Mary Caine, author of The Glastonbury Zodiac ~

I am pleased that my friend Laurence Main is writing this guide to Somerset, especially as it includes my particular preoccupation, the Glastonbury Zodiac – that collection of landscape features around Glastonbury that we can associate with the celestial zodiac. It is one thing to read about these Giant figures, which can give such insight into our place and purpose in life, and have the power to unify all faiths into a single cosmological whole, but it is quite another experience to walk amongst them with their message in mind. Not only has the landscape a beauty all its own, dominated by Glastonbury's extraordinary Tor, but magical things can happen here which revive one's childhood sense of wonder. The pilgrim (of whatever faith or none) in the Vale of Avalon is liable before long to feel that he is more than half out of this world.

Katharine Maltwood, the sculptress who discovered (or rediscovered) this Zodiac, made the startling claim that it was the original Round Table in Avalon, with Arthur and his chief knights still seated about it as the 12 signs. The Zodiac indicates the sun's path through the year, so Arthur is the sun-king of this circle. But as the sun must decline nightly and annually, he is here denoted by Sagittarius' wintry sign, as befits the tragic 'Morte d'Arthur'. Leo is Lancelot, peerless knight of high summer. All Arthurian and Grail legends originate, she asserted, from this great Star-Temple, already ancient in Arthurian times. The knights' Quest for the hidden Grail was both an inner search and an outer one for those hidden figures, for though the Celtic memory of them was preserved in Glastonbury Abbey, their shape and exact location was already lost in the mists of time. So the knights were searching for their own sun-signs – Themselves!

She assigned Aquarius to Perceval, the boy from the backwoods who finally achieved the Grail-quest, and in the legends he is given the significant name of 'Par-lui-fet' – he who makes or renews himself, like the phoenix. The Grail Mysteries are successors to those more ancient, for a hymn to Egyptian Ra also invokes him as 'Thou, self-begotten, who didst give birth to thyself'.

In my experience these Mysteries are still very much alive in Avalon and will speak by coincidence and miracle to pilgrims who venture on these paths. Put them to the test yourself!

Mary Caine

Contents

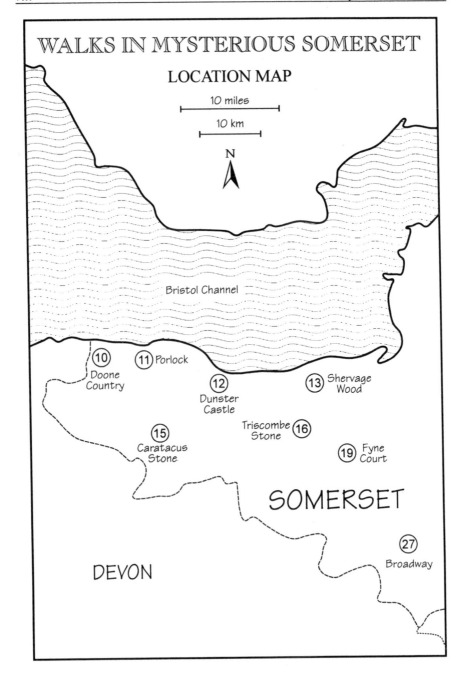

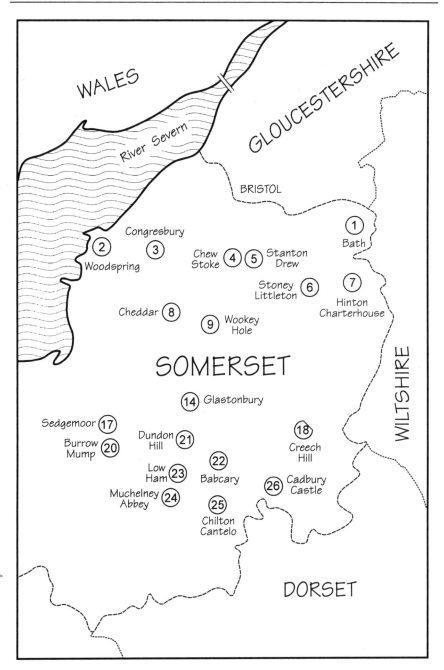

Introduction

This is a book of walks in Somerset averaging six miles in length, from and to places which represent the great store of legend, magic, mystery and sense of belonging to the living land that can still be perceived by the rambler. It has two aims. One is to open the eyes of the walker to the nature of the land he or she sets foot on, so that mutual love can be exchanged and humankind can shake itself awake to the need to live in harmony with Mother Earth. The other is to invite those armchair followers of the New Age fashion and even those most worthy souls who tend their organic or veganic gardens to embrace a little bit more of their planet, to let their soft feet inform remote areas that they are not neglected and to allow places where the spirit has survived more strongly to work through us.

None of these walks exceeds 10 miles in length (but some can be linked together to make longer routes), yet the hills and moors of Somerset offer enough of a challenge to stimulate the adventurous. Even the wetlands of the Levels contribute to the complete picture. There is a wealth of wonderful scenery and the contrast with the noisy corridors containing the motorists is clear. The motorcar is one of the chief enemies of the living earth and it makes a nonsense of your reverence for nature if you add to the pollution and demand for more roads. The local bus or train will be glad of your support. Details of public transport are given for each walk. Public transport allows the freedom of following linear routes (a few of which are included in this book) with bus stops or railway stations at each end.

Somerset history

There's much more to this book than walks. There are the history and local legends of this ancient area to discover. For example, how did the old county, now divided into three parts by the bureaucrats, acquire its name? Legend states that this was the seat of the Sumers, from Sumeria, which certainly bears a similarity to 'Somerset'. The legend may have been inspired by the historical fact that the Phoenicians, relatively near neighbours, came here to trade for local metals. The Sumers were known to be great astrologers and, perhaps coincidentally, Somerset is the home of the enigmatic landscape feature known as the Glastonbury Zodiac (see the Foreword to this book and Walk 14). As a final coincidental link, the original term for a somersault, possibly symbolising the turning wheel of the zodiac, was a 'somerset'.

About the Walks

Each walk is organised in the same way, using three sections:

The first section gives you the 'bare bones' of the walk - its route, the length, maps to take with you and so on. This will help you to select the walks to suit your ability or time available.

The next section – 'Round andAbout' – gives you an historical anecdote, a spooky tale or some interesting folklore associated with the area in which you are walking. This adds a great deal to each walk, so be sure to read it. There's far more to discover on the walks than can be described here, and there's often more than one explanation for any mysterious events that are described. Make up your own mind!

The final section is the walk itself. Numbered points are used and these relate to the sketch maps provided to help you along your way. Please remember, however, that the sketch maps are not a replacement for the Ordnance Survey map(s) recommended at the start of the walk

What you'll find on the walks

There's much to discover on these 'mysterious walks'. Ley lines feature frequently and make an early appearance in Walk2, while ancient stone circles are explored in Walk 5.

Reincarnation is investigated in Walks 8 and 17; dragons are tamed in walk 12 and the setting of the fictional Frankenstein is explored during Walk 19. Those of a nervous disposition should think twice before embarking on Walk 16, where the Devil rides out!

In Walk 9 you'll read of Samuel Taylor Coleridge – a poet inspired by this area. He had Wookey Hole in mind when composing *Kubla Khan*, with its 'caverns measureless to man'. Coleridge introduced William Wordsworth and his sister Dorothy to the Quantocks, a word in the Celtic language which signifies a rim. This is exactly what they appear to be when seen from the Somerset Levels. The prehistoric ridgeway along the tops of the hills is followed on stormy nights by the Wild Hunt (see Walk 16) when the devil himself is said to ride a black steed at the head of a pack of Wish-Hounds – the spirits of the eternally damned.

Walk 10 takes you west of Minehead to Exmoor, whose bleak and rugged land holds the rare beauty of wilderness. A National Park, its heights provide splendid views across the Bristol Channel to South Wales, bringing reminders of a common link with King Arthur, the legendary British ruler. The mysterious Doone family are featured in this excellent walk.

Glastonbury, its tor and connections with both Celtic and early Christian history are explored in detail in Walk 14. If you do no other walk in this book, you must tackle this one. Steeped in legends, Glastonbury is the focus of interest for all those followers of New Age beliefs – or even the mildly curious.

Alfred found inspiration when brought to the test at Athelney (Walk 20), but the Duke of Monmouth lost his head. Did John Fletcher die at the Battle of Sedgemoor in 1685 and was he reincarnated as E.W. Ryall in the 20th century, as recounted in Walk 8? Make up your own mind whilst wandering around places featured in the book 'Second Time Round'.

On Walk 21 we encounter the greatest Somerset legend of all, concerning Joseph of Arimathea, who was said to have been entrusted with the care of the young Jesus by his niece, Mary. It is claimed that Joseph was a tin trader who brought Jesus to Glastonbury, where the druids accepted Him and the first Christian church was alleged to have been built by Jesus' own hands. There are also claims that after the crucifixion, Mary, the mother of Jesus, came to Glastonbury with Joseph of Arimathea and is now said to lie buried in the grounds of the ruined abbey. Decide for yourself: walk in the Mendips, the very hills which inspired William Blake – himself descended from a Somerset family and an Archdruid – to write of 'the Holy Lamb of God' on these 'mountains green'.

Having gained confidence by following routes from a book, go out and explore Somerset on your own with the aid of those more precious keys to enjoying the countryside, the Ordnance Survey maps. Explorers have replaced the smaller Pathfinders at the valuable scale of 1:25 000 (2½ inches to one mile).

The Ramblers' Association

Each walk in this book follows rights of way to which you, as a member of the public, have unrestricted access. Should you come across any problems, send full details (including grid references) to: The Ramblers' Association, 1/5 Wandsworth Road, London, SW8 2XX, tel. 0171 339 8500. Better still, join the Ramblers, go out on their group walks and volunteer to help deal with path problems yourself.

The Ley Hunter

Many people believe in ley lines, perhaps as traditional routes that linked hillforts, churches and other locations across the countryside. Some attribute a spiritual dimension to them. Enthusiastic ley hunters believe that significant leys run through Somerset. Keep up to date with the latest thinking on these spirit paths, death roads or Old Straight Tracks by reading The Ley Hunter, PO Box 180, Stroud, Gloucestershire, GL5 1YH; tel. 0402 998208.

Pendragon

Somerset has strong links with King Arthur. A rich debate about exact locations and identities can be followed in the specialist journal of the Pendragon Society, c/o John and Linda Ford, 41 Ridge Street, Watford, Herts, WD2 5BL.

The Country Code

+ Guard against all risk of fire.

+ Fasten all gates (N.B. This is the official advice. In practice, farmers usually leave gates open on purpose, so that sheep can reach water etc., so leave gates as you find them.)

+ Keep dogs under proper control.

+ Avoid damaging fences, hedges and walls.

+ Keep to paths across farmland.

+ Leave no litter.

+ Safeguard water supplies.

+ Protect wildlife, wild plants and trees.

+ Go carefully on country roads.

+ Respect the life of the countryside.

1. Bath

Route: Elmhurst – Little Solsbury Hillfort – Batheaston – Toll Bridge – Kennet and Avon Canal – Bath

Distance: 6 miles. Strenuous at first, then easy. Linear route with bus stops at both ends.

Maps: O.S. Explorer 155 Bristol and Bath; O.S. Landranger 172 Bristol and Bath.

Start: No. 13 bus terminus in Catherine Way, Elmhurst (ST781680).

Finish: Bus station, Bath (ST752644).

Access: Bath City bus no. 13 runs to the start of this walk in Elmhurst from Bath bus station (tel. 0117 955 5111 for bus details). Bath has a railway station on the line between Bristol and London (tel. 0345 484950 about train services).

Round and About

Mount Badon and King Arthur

Mount Badon was the alleged scene of King Arthur's twelfth battle. It was a memorable victory in which the British crushed the Saxons and secured a generation's peace. According to Nennius, a historian monk who lived around 800, Arthur himself single-handedly slew 960 men in one day – a formidable number! The battle took place in the early sixth century, probably in 516 or 518. There are other candidates for its site, including Baydon near Swindon (see *Walks in Mysterious Wiltshire* in this series). Bath is the clear favourite of Chris Barber and David Pykitt, authors of *Journey to Avalon*. As the Caer Baddon of the Britons, its 'dd' was pronounced 'th', thus Badon is easily linked to Bath. To the Romans, this was *Aquae Sulis*, named after the British Goddess of the Springs, Sulis, whom the Romans equated with Minerva, goddess of healing. Nennius wrote of the 'baths of Ba-

Bath Abbey

don' being 'in the country of the Hwicce'. The Hwicce were the Cotswold branch of the Gewissei whose leader was Cerdic, British ally of the Jutes and Saxons. Geoffrey of Monmouth's *History of the Kings of Britain* tells how Arthur's shield bore 'a likeness of the Blessed Mary, Mother of God' (a Christian account of an icon of the Goddess) and that the Saxons occupied a hill which Arthur and his army climbed. Geoffrey recorded that 'Cheldric ... when he saw the danger threatening his men, immediately turned in flight with what troops were left to him'. Was this Cerdic, fleeing from Arthur? Was this the hill occupied by Saxons (allies of Cerdic) and taken by Arthur that crowned by a hillfort near the start of this walk, Little Solsbury Hill?

Healing Waters

The healing springs of Bath were, according to legend, found by Bladud. He was the eldest son of Lud Hudibras, a descendant of Brutus, and lived in the ninth century BC. His prospects were threatened when he contracted leprosy and had to leave court. Becoming a swineherd in north Somerset, he infected the pigs with his leprosy. They led Bladud to hot springs in a swamp where the water restored their health. Bladud copied their cure and eventually came to the throne. He set up his court at Caer Baddon and dedicated the springs to the goddess Sul.

Bladud's inquisitive mind led to him making a pair of wings and attempting to fly from the summit of Little Solsbury Hill. He fell to his death, to be succeeded by his son, Lear (of Shakespeare fame). One story is that when he fell, Bladud landed in (and, even, discovered) the famous baths. This may, of course, be a reference to spirit flight.

Loyal to the Royals

Bath's royal connections have been maintained over the centuries. The first king of all England was crowned here in 973. Another King, an Oliver King, secretary to Henry VII and Bishop of Bath, rebuilt the Abbey as a result of a dream. He had a vision of angels ascending and descending between heaven and earth with the aid of a ladder.

The Walk

1. With the road on your right, walk away from Bath (going north). Ignore the continuation of Catherine Way forking right. Go ahead along a road, which is a dead end for motorists. Pedestrians can join Steway Lane and go left with it. Ignore a signposted footpath (part of the Limestone Link) on your right, go ahead across a bridge and turn left at a road junction. Pass the Church of St John the Baptist on your right, pass a lane on your right and immediately after it bear right to follow the public footpath signposted for Bailbrook. This path soon emerges into a field where you go left, walking with a hedge on your left. Continue over a stile, climb to join a road and turn right up this. Fork right up a lane which ends in a gate giving access to Little Solsbury Hill. Go ahead to explore the hillfort which crowns the summit.

2. Retrace your steps down the lane and road (Solsbury Lane) but this time ignore the footpath back to the church on your left and go ahead to a road junction. Go right and immediately bear left down an enclosed path to Batheaston High Street. Cross this road carefully, go left and reach a bus shelter. Turn sharply right along a signposted path. Walk with the River Avon on your left, going downstream.

3. Turn left over a toll bridge (free for pedestrians in 1998), passing the waterwheel of an old mill on your left. Continue with this road to cross bridges over the A4 and the railway. Do not cross a bridge over the Kennet and Avon Canal. When you approach it, turn right to walk along the towpath with the canal on your left.

4. Reach a bridge carrying a road over the canal. Leave the towpath to go right down Beckford Road, immediately crossing the railway and passing Beckford Gardens on your right. Bear left downhill and go left along Sydney Place with Sydney Gardens and the Holburne Museum on your left and the house

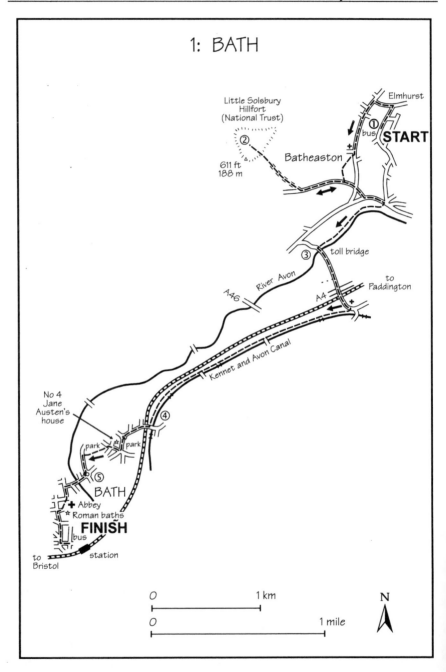

(no 4) where Jane Austen lived from 1801 to 1805 on your right. Turn right along Sutton Street. Go ahead with the path through Henrietta Park, aiming for its far-left corner (where there is a Garden for the Blind). Turn left along Henrietta Street.

5. Go right at Laura Place to follow Argyle Street into Bridge Street. Turn left along High Street to reach the Abbey. Bear right in the corner to pass the front of the Abbey and go left to pass the Roman Baths on your left. Continue to the shopping centre and bear left for the bus station.

2. Woodspring

Route: Sand Bay – Sand Point – Woodspring Priory – Kewstoke – Worlebury Hill – Weston-super-Mare

Distance: 10 miles. Strenuous at times. Linear route with bus stops at both ends.

Maps: O.S. Pathfinder 1181 Weston-super-Mare; O.S. Explorer 153 Weston-super-Mare and Bleadon Hill; O.S. Landranger 181 Weston-super-Mare and Bridgwater.

Start: Sand Bay bus terminus (no. 100 in summer, no. 1 in winter), (ST332646).

Finish: Grand Pier, Weston-super-Mare (ST317614).

Access: Bus no. 100 (normally operated by open-top buses) runs from Weston-super-Mare Grand Pier to Sandy Bay in the summer. This becomes bus no. 1 in the winter (tel. 0117 955 3231 about buses). Weston-super-Mare has a railway station on the line between Bristol and Taunton (tel. 0345 484950 about trains).

Round and About

A Funeral Passage?

Rhines or rhynes (pronounced 'reens') are drainage channels. There is a curiously straight one running at an angle from ST342653 to ST339643, a distance of one kilometre (0.6 miles). Extending this line southwards, it reaches Worlesbury Hill near the ancient church at Kewstoke and the Monks Steps. There are examples of coffin ways or corpse paths running straight through the land, or keeping as close as possible to the terrain-oblivious spirit path, but this could well be a coffin rhyne. Its diagonal nature runs against the pattern of all the other rhynes (check the O.S. Pathfinder or Explorer map). Couple this fact with the legend, recorded by Phil Quinn in *The Ley Hunter* no. 128, that the monks used a secret passageway to carry their dead to spring Priory from Worlebury Hill and this may well be a watery spirit path through the levels of Sand Bay. Such routes were 'dead straight', as Paul Devereux has commented on in *Shamanism and the Mystery Lines.* In this case we also have the symbolism of the dead being ferried by boat (navigated by hooded figures), just as people are said to dream of moving across a body of water when going between worlds in dreams at sacred sites during special periods (that's if they're pure enough to deserve a boat – some have to swim for it!). The monks of Glastonbury Abbey were said to have rowed their dead to Nyland Hill. It does seem strange for the monks of Woodspring to arrange to die on Worlebury Hill, but there is a magical element to this place (often the case with peninsulas, as, indeed, with Sand Point, which bears a tumulus).

Fortified resistance

The hillfort on Worlebury Hill was probably a centre of resistance by a southern section of the Dobunni tribe to the Roman invasion in AD43. Its walls of loose stone and some of its many storage pits can be seen on this walk. Perhaps the skeletons found there were of the final defenders against the Romans. A coin hoard suggests the hillfort was re-occupied by the time of King Arthur (around AD 500). The sixth-century Celtic St Kew was also here, founding his place of prayer on the site of what is now St Paul's Church, Kewstoke. Kewstoke could also be derived from the ancient British words for boat and station – reinforcing the coffin rhyne idea, with the rhyne presumably extending to the church at the foot of Monks Steps, being the station for the boat which carried the corpse. St Kew was Docwin, otherwise known as Cyngar (founder of Congresbury, Walk 3) and according to Chris Barber and David Pykitt in *Journey to Avalon* may have been the son of Gildas the historian. Elissa Henken argues in *Traditions of the Welsh Saints* that Cyngar was the grandson of Cattw (the Cadwy who ruled Somerset with Arthur, see Dunster Castle, Walk 12). Cyngar was also called Doccuinus (Docwin) because he taught (*docebat*).

The Walk

1. Go right from the no. 100 bus terminus at Sand Bay, towards the sea, turning right at the end of Sand Road and going ahead along Beach Road (a No Through Road), keeping the sea on your left. Alternative, unofficial paths exist on your left, parallel to the road and on the beach. Notice the islands of Steep Holm and Flat Holm in the Bristol Channel away to your left, with the coastline of South Wales beyond them. Reach the National Trust car park at the end of Beach Road. Bear left up steps and climb with a path past shrubland to a trig point and a tumulus. Go left, westwards, to enjoy the view from Sand Point with Sand Bay on your left.

2. Retrace your steps to the trig point, with Sand Bay now on your right. Continue with the Bristol Channel on your left, going ahead through grassland and taking a gate in a wall ahead. Cross a ladder-stile to the left of a gate in the next wall. Go ahead with a wall on your right, pass a private road on your right, continue ahead for another 500 metres (540 yards), then turn right through a kissing-gate in the corner. Go ahead along the left-hand edge of a field, take a waymarked gap into the next field and keep to its left-hand edge until a waymarked gate. Bear left through this to follow a path to another National Trust car park.

3. Go right along the access lane and bear left at a junction with the lane coming from Woodspring Farm. When level with the buildings of Culm Farm away to your left, turn right to take a signposted public bridleway. This hedged old green lane emerges at a gate in a corner ahead (which you do not take) and a rhyne or drainage channel beyond it.

4. Bear left to walk with this (corpse?) rhyne on your right, then divert from it to follow the hedged path. Turn left at a track junction. When this firm track bears left, turn right to follow a

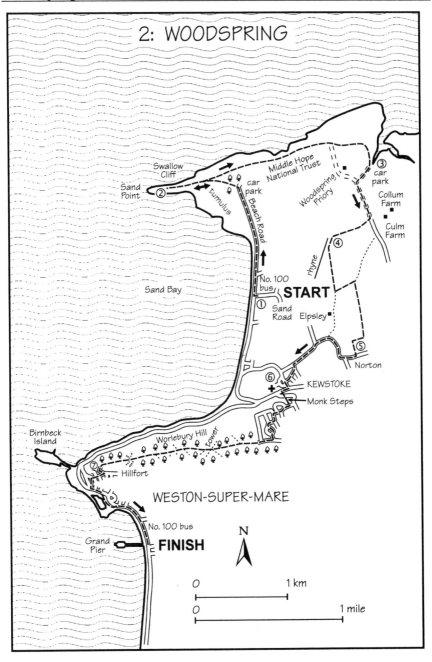

grassy path. This acquires a metalled surface as it bears right, then left to join a road.

5. Go right along the road, pass a turning on your left, take a bend on your right and bear left to pass the drive to Elmsley Nursery on your right. Fork left at the next road junction. Turn left up Kewside and go left up Crookes Lane. Bear right along Kewstoke Road to reach St Paul's Church on your right.

6. Cross the road from the church to go up steps leading to a steep path. Cross a very high step stile in a wall, go ahead across a road and up Monks Steps. Emerge at a bus stop in Woodspring Avenue and go right, passing Spring Close on your right. Turn left along Furze Road and follow it as it bends right (ignoring Hillcroft Close ahead). Go left along Worlebury Park Road, passing an island of trees to reach Worlebury Hill Road. Go right, either along this road or with a woodland path parallel to it and continue straight ahead with the main track through the woodland of Worlebury Hill. Reach a water tower on your right and go ahead along the main woodland track. When the bridleway bears right, fork left to follow the footpath to the ramparts and tumbled stone walls of Worlebury Hillfort. Continue to a small clearing where another path goes left downhill.

7. Turn left to take the path downhill and emerge in Trinity Road. Go left down this, turn right along South Road and bear left down Madeira Road. Go left along Birnbeck Road and soon take a path on your right to pass a bandstand and follow Marine Parade, with the sea on your right, all the way back to Weston-super-Mare's Grand Pier.

3. Congresbury

Route: Congresbury – Wrington Hill – Wrington – Congresbury

Distance: 7 miles. Moderate.

Maps: O.S. Pathfinder 1182 Yatton and Chew Magna; O.S. Explorer 154 Bristol West and Portishead; O.S. Landranger 172 Bristol and Bath.

Start: Bus shelter on the northern side of Congresbury Bridge, Congresbury (ST438639).

Access: Buses numbers XI, 350, 351, 352 and 353 run through Congresbury on their way between Bristol and Weston-super-Mare (tel. 0117 955 3231 for details).

Round and About

St Congar

Congresbury's church is dedicated to St Andrew and was consecrated in 1215. This is a much older sacred site, however, as witnessed by an ancient yew in the churchyard. This is known as St Congar's walking-stick. The Saxon conquerors of Somerset weren't too sure who St Congar was, but they knew this place was special. There had been an ancient settlement just to the north on Cadbury Hill (another of Somerset's Cadbury Castles), followed by a Roman villa. This Cadbury Castle, like the one at South Cadbury, was re-occupied in Arthurian times. This was the period when Congar, or Cyngar, who is also met on Walk 2 (Woodspring) came here. Legend states how he dreamt of a wild boar. Taking this to be a sign, when he did see a wild boar resting at this spot he knew to found a Celtic monastery (very different from the Roman sort!) here. In the process, marshland was turned into field and meadow. The bishop's see was removed to Wells in 721.

The Walk

1. With your back to the bus shelter, go right, away from the bridge. Soon fork right up Kent Road. When this approaches the A370 on your left, bear right along Wrington Lane.

2. At the end of Wrington Lane, go left and almost immediately right to take the drive to The Woodlands. Fork left along the signposted public footpath. Ignore a gate into woodland on your left. Go ahead over a stile and follow the public path which soon enters the wood. The path becomes a roughly-metalled track after Woolmers. Bear left with this to emerge at a road.

3. Go right up the road (Wrington Hill), passing through woodland and ignoring a track to Bracken Hill on your right. Descend to a house called Oaklands on your right and turn right along a signposted public bridleway. This is a hedged, muddy, track called Bullhouse Lane. Follow it down to Wrington.

4. Turn left along Roper's Lane and after 45 metres (50 yards), just before Yeoman's Orchard, turn right down a walled path. Go left along a road into Wrington and pass the Plough Inn on your right. Bear right to follow Broad Street. Go straight ahead in the corner and fork right, away from the church on your left, to take Ladywell. After 45 metres (50 yards) turn right along a signposted public footpath. This enclosed path emerges through a kissing-gate into an open field.

5. Turn left to walk with a hedge on your left. When the hedge turns left, go straight ahead to cross a stile in the hedge opposite. Walk with a hedge on your right in the next field. Turn right over a stile beside a gate, turn left immediately and go ahead over a stile to the right of a gate in the corner. Continue with a hedge on your left, pass under power lines, then turn left over a stile to turn right with the waymarked Two Rivers

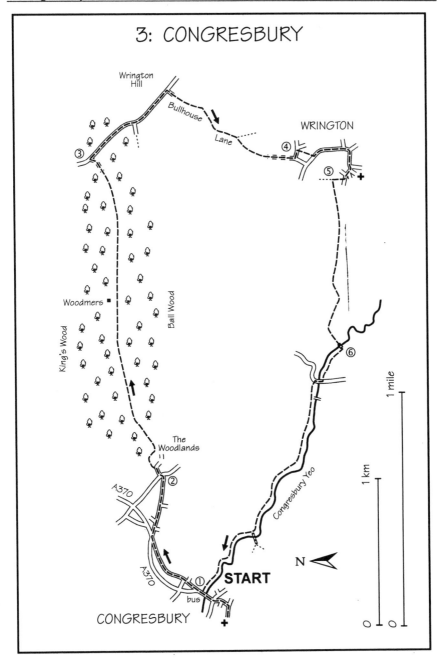

3: CONGRESBURY

Way, following a hedge on your right. Go ahead over a stile to the left of an iron gate and bear half-left through the next field, ignoring a gate in the hedge on your right. Take a gate in the hedge ahead (ignoring the indented corner to the right of it) and walk with a hedge on your right to a stile in the next corner. Go left through the following field and cross a footbridge over a river, the Congresbury Yeo.

5. Turn right to walk downstream with the river on your right. Reach a road, turn right to cross a bridge over the river and immediately turn left to walk with the river on your left. Ignore footbridges across the river as you continue along the northern bank of the Congresbury Yeo back into Congresbury. Divert left over the Congresbury Bridge and go ahead up Broad Street. Turn right at Paul's Causeway to reach St Andrew's Church. Retrace your steps over Congresbury Bridge to the bus stop.

St Andrew's church, Congresbury

4. Chew Stoke

Route: Chew Magna – Two Rivers Way – Chew Valley Lake – Chew Stoke – Pagans Hill – Chew Magna.

Distance: 5 miles. Moderate.

Maps: O.S. Explorer 155 Bristol and Bath; O.S. Landranger 172 Bristol and Bath.

Start: Post Office, Chew Magna (ST576632).

Access: Buses to Chew Magna include no. 673 from Bristol (tel. 0117 955 5111 for details).

Round and About

Molly's Spirit Flight

Molly N was an eccentric woman (although she dressed as a man) whose spirit flight south from Bristol featured in an article by Phil Quinn in *The Ley Hunter* no. 126. This possible ley or spirit path skirted the foot of Pagans Hill, once occupied by an octagonal Roman temple and votive well. An ancient burial path led south to St Andrew's Church, Chew Stoke, using Pilgrims Way as a link. The church bells were also taken along Pilgrims Way when transported for repairs. Now lost to the south of the church is a stone circle (ST559616) and St Anthony's Well (ST559613). St Andrew's Church, Chew Stoke, used to be dedicated to St Wigefort. It was an important centre of the cult of 'Maid Uncumber'. Represented as a bearded woman (no wonder old Molly N dressed as a man!), she offered hope to women wishing to rid themselves of their husbands. Chew Valley Lake is a reservoir opened by Queen Elizabeth II on 17 April, 1956. It covers a Roman road and villa, including evidence of iron-working and lime-burning. The medieval nunnery of St Cross was on the western shore.

The Walk

1. With your back to Chew Magna Post Office, go right, soon ignoring a turning on your right. Look out for a public footpath sign high up on a pole, pointing left. Turn left to cross the road carefully and take a narrow, enclosed, path. This is part of the Two Rivers Way.

2. Descend to a footbridge, turn left across it, bear right and cross a second footbridge. Turn right immediately along an access path to a house on your right, cross a stile next to a gate on your left and turn right along the right-hand side of a field.

3. Go ahead along the waymarked Two Rivers Way, crossing a stile and walking along the right-hand side of the next field. Go ahead over a stone-slab bridge, continue through another field to cross a stile ahead and follow a hedge on your left. Take a stile beside a gate in the corner, go through the middle of the next field and take a footbridge to follow a woodland path.

4. Turn left along a lane and go right when it joins a road (Denny Lane). Descend to a junction and turn right to very soon find Chew Valley Lake (a reservoir) on your left. Notice a track signposted as a public path coming sharply from your right. Go ahead 25 metres (27 yards).

5. Turn right over a stile to enter a corner of a field and go ahead beside a hedge on your left. Continue over a footbridge and along an enclosed path to reach a road (Chew Lane). Go left and keep straight ahead at a crossroads to follow Pilgrims Way. Pass Scot Lane on your right (for now), bear left, then turn right along Church Lane to reach St Andrew's Church, Church Stoke.

6. Go back down Church Lane, turn left but this time fork left up Scot Lane. Bear right with this lane as it climbs to a junction.

Bear right at the end of Scot Lane, but first cast your eye over Pagans Hill on your left. Turn right at a road junction for **90 metres (100 yards)**.

7. Turn left along Chillyhill Lane, which deteriorates to a muddy green lane before becoming metalled again as it approaches the main road into Chew Magna. Go right to return to the Post Office and bus stop.

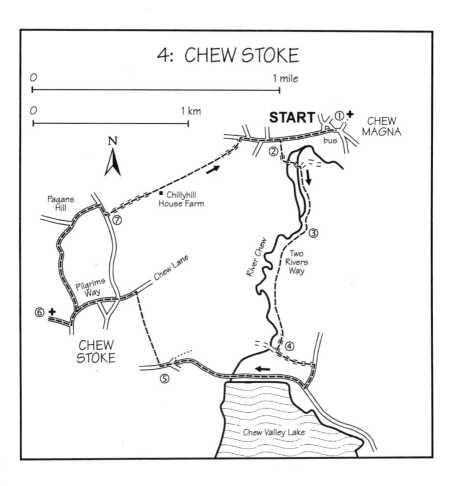

5. Stanton Drew

Route: Chew Magna – Three Peaks Walk – Two Rivers Way – The Cove – Stanton Drew Stone Circles – Norton Lane – Chew Magna

Distance: 5½ miles. Strenuous.

Maps: O.S. Explorer 155 Bristol and Bath; O.S. Landranger 172 Bristol and Bath.

Start: Post Office, Chew Magna (ST576632).

Access: Buses to Chew Magna include no. 673 from Bristol (tel. 0117 955 5111 for details).

Round and About

Wedding Rings

The stone circles of Stanton Drew date from about 2500 BC. Legend links the stone circles to a wedding party held on a Midsummer's Eve that was turned to stone for not calling a halt to its dancing so as not to intrude on the Sabbath. The folk memory of a connection with fertility and the summer solstice may well be true.

Also in Stanton Drew, in 1997 amazing discoveries were made by archaeologists using a magnetometer (a highly sensitive instrument for measuring the earth's magnetism) to 'X-ray' the ground. They found the world's largest prehistoric building, dating to about 3000 BC, with a diameter of 95 metres (104 yards). Made of wood, it may or may not have had a roof (perhaps with a central skylight).

The Great Circle stands above the earlier, huge, wooden structure and the main entrance of the newly-discovered building faced towards the summer solstice sunrise. Facing in the same direction, a line (possibly a ley) can be traced at an angle of about 50 degrees running through the cove, the centre of the Great Circle and the smaller north-east circle. Our Stone Age ancestors were more sophisticated than previously thought!

The Great circle is the second largest of its kind, exceeded only by Avebury, while the north-east circle is the most complete of the three here. The isolated south-west circle may be on a ley running through it, the Great circle and a standing stone (now recumbent) called Hauteville's Quoit, to the north.

The three stones of the Cove (two still standing and one flat and broken into two) are closest to the church, dedicated to St Mary. Of course, it's obvious why all these stones (and before them the wooden structure) are here – their site is conveniently close to the Druid's Arms pub!

There is an admission charge to Stanton Drew Stone Circles.

Stanton Drew

The Walk

1. With your back to Chew Magna Post Office, go left to the end of south parade and bear left through the churchyard, passing St Andrew's church, Chew Magna, on your left. Bear right to cross a bridge and turn right. Ignore a footbridge on your right and follow North Chew Terrace to its end. Go straight ahead across a road junction and follow the signposted by-way. Walk with a high wall on your right and turn right with this wall to reach the B3130 road.

2. Go left for 45 metres (50 yards) and turn right along Sandy Lane, which forms part of the waymarked Three Peaks Walk. Cross a bridge over the River Chew and bear right to pass a place called Paradise. Go ahead along the old green, perhaps muddy, lane. This becomes metalled as it approaches Stanton Drew (and now forms part of the Two Rivers Way). Go right in the village to pass the Druids Arms pub on your left and reach The Cove (customers of the pub may go up the steps on your left to inspect these standing stones).

3. Return along the road to pass the Druids Arms pub on your right. Bear right at the junction and fork right. Pass Court Cottage on your left to follow the signposted access lane to Stanton Drew Stone Circles. After visiting these, return to the road and go right to follow it across a bridge over the River Chew. Reach a T-junction with an attractive old toll-house in a road island at its centre. Go right for a few paces.

4. Turn left to take the signposted footpath immediately before a garage. This goes up steps to cross a stile. Go ahead to cross a stile in the hedge ahead, keep climbing with a hedge on our left and take a stile in the top left-hand corner. Climb to a stile in the hedge about 90 metres (100 yards) to the right of the corner formed with the hedge coming up on your left. Maintain this direction to go ahead over another stile in the next hedge ahead, again about 90 metres (100 yards) from the corner on

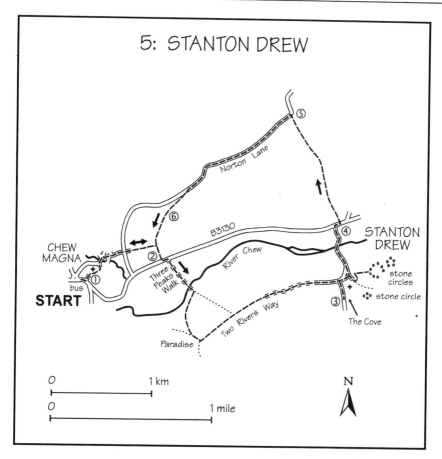

5: STANTON DREW

Norton Lane

⑤

CHEW
MAGNA

⑥

B3130

River Chew

②

Three Peaks Walk

bus

START

①

④ STANTON
DREW

••• stone
circles

•••• stone circle

③

Two Rivers Way

The Cove

Paradise

0 ——————— 1 km

0 ——————————————— 1 mile

N

▲

your left. Continue beside a hedge on your right, cross a stile
in the corner ahead and bear very slightly right through the
next field to take a stile giving access to a road (Norton Lane).

5. Go left along Norton Lane. Look out for a public footpath signpost on your left. Turn left over a stile and immediately turn
right along the top of this field.

6. Cross a stile in the hedge ahead and bear left down the next
field to a stile in its far bottom left corner. Cross this and bear
right to the bottom right corner of the following field. Take a

gate into another field, walk along its right-hand edge for 45 metres (50 yards) and cross a waymarked stile beside a gate. Turn right to retrace your steps along the by-way of your outward route, this time walking with the high wall on your left. Continue along North Chew Terrace, bear left through the chruch yard and go right to return to the bus stop in chew Magna.

6. Stoney Littleton Long Barrow

Route: Peasedown St John – White Ox Mead – Wellow – Stoney Littleton Long Barrow – Hang Hill – Peasedown St John

Distance: 7½ miles. Moderate.

Maps: O.S. Explorer 5 Mendip Hills East; O.S. Landranger 172 Bristol and Bath.

Start: Red Post Inn, Peasedown St John (ST698572).

Access: Buses run to the Red Post Inn, Peasedown St John, from Bath (nos. 173, 176 and 184), Wells (no. 173), Shepton Mallett (no. 176) and Frome (no. 184). Tel. 0117 955 3231 for details.

Round and About

An Injured Tomb

A plaque on the right side of the entrance to Stoney Littleton Long Barrow records how it was restored in 1858 with 'scrupulous exactness, after being much injured' due to 'the lapse of time or the carelessness of its former proprietors'. A modern notice on the door recently placed across the entrance to this ancient long barrow betrays the fact that it is still not being looked after properly. English Heritage have denied access to its interior (most importantly, even to the sun) because they can't afford to make necessary repairs to the roofs of the chamber and the passage. This is a great shame as the midwinter sunrise shines through this long barrow's entrance and illuminates two prominent ammonite casts in the stones. There is an information board near the gate in the fence surrounding the long barrow. This is on its western side (on the left as you face the entrance). There are parallels here with Newgrange in Ireland. For more information, read *The Boyne Valley Vision* and *The Stars and the Stones* by Martin Brennan, also *Pi in the, Sky* by Michael Poynder.

The Walk

1. Face the Red Post Inn, go right and immediately turn left along Wellow Lane. This is joined by a new road coming sharply from your right and passes estate roads on your left, including Braysdown Lane. A new road runs parallel on your right. Go ahead along the pavement of a No Through Road and continue with a path towards a roundabout. Turn right to cross the new road, passing the roundabout on your left. Bear right along the road for Wellow. Pass a signposted by-way which comes in sharply on your right. Go ahead 45 metres (50 yards).

2. Turn left to cross a stile beside a gate and follow a signposted public footpath. This is enclosed, with a hedge on your right and a fence on your left at first, then there is a hedge on both sides. Emerge to cross a road and take the signposted by-way ahead. This goes through a gate and follows the left-hand sides of three fields.

3. Go ahead across a hedged public footpath and continue along the hedged track. Pass the interestingly-named White Ox Mead (shamans experienced visionary dreams whilst lying on ox-hides, as in *The Mabinogion* story of *The Dream of Rhonabwy*) on your left. Another hedged track climbs sharply from your left to join yours. Go ahead, passing under power lines and by the site of a Roman villa near a clump of trees on the hillside sloping down on your right. Reach a road at a junction.

4. Turn right downhill along the road into Wellow. In the centre of this village, where there is a telephone box on your right, bear left to cross the street. Turn right down a narrow lane, passing the Fox and Badger pub on your left. When this lane ends at a gate, continue down a path and cross a bridge over the Wellow Brook.

5. Go right with a raised causeway and join the lane running be-

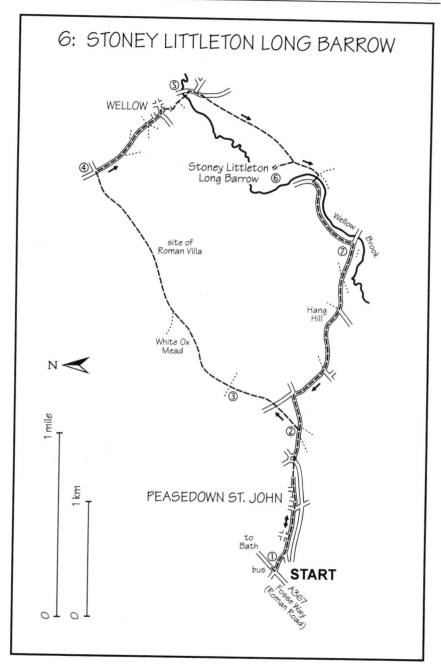

6: STONEY LITTLETON LONG BARROW

WELLOW

⑤

④

Stoney Littleton
Long Barrow ⑥

Wellow

Brook

site of
Roman Villa

⑦

Hang
Hill

White Ox
Mead

③

N

②

1 mile

1 km

PEASEDOWN ST. JOHN

to
Bath

①

bus

START

A367
Fosse Way
(Roman Road)

low it. Bear right when this lane forks and about 45 metres (50 yards) later, bear right to leave the lane and follow a hedged path which may be muddy in places. Pass under power lines, emerge through a gate and go ahead through a field. A hedge comes from your left to meet the path. It turns, so that you continue with a hedge on your left. Reach a gate on your left but do not take it yet. Firstly, turn right to visit Stoney Littleton Long Barrow.

Stoney Littleton Long Barrow

6. Retrace your steps from the long barrow to the gate which was on your left. Go through it and bear right beside the hedge on your right. Descend to the bottom right corner, where you cross a stile and walk along the right-hand edge of the next field, going upstream with the Wellow Brook on your right. Turn right to cross a footbridge over this. Go left along a signposted, metalled, by-way and follow it to a junction with a road.

7. Turn right along the road, climb Hang Hill and ignore two turnings on your left. Reach a crossroads and turn left along a road which soon brings you back to the stile you crossed at point 2. Go ahead to retrace your steps to the Red Post Inn.

7. Hinton Charterhouse

Route: Hinton Charterhouse — Hinton Priory — Pipehouse — Midford Hill — Hinton Priory — Church of St John the Baptist — Hinton Charterhouse

Distance: 3½ miles. Easy.

Maps: O.S. Explorer 5 Mendip Hills East; O.S. Landranger 172 Bristol and Bath.

Start: The Stag Inn, Hinton Charterhouse (ST772582).

Access: Bus no. 267 (Bath-Frome) serves Hinton Charterhouse. Tel. 0117 955511 for details.

Round and About

A Secret Tunnel

Hinton means 'high ground', while Charterhouse refers to the Carthusian priory located here in the Middle Ages. Its founder was Ela, Countess of Salisbury and wife of William Longspee, the son of King Henry II by his mistress Fair Rosamund Clifford (find out about Fair Roz in *Walks in Mysterious Oxfordshire* in this series). Ela remained faithful to her husband while he was away for many years campaigning in France. When he died, he became the first man to be buried in Salisbury Cathedral. Ela waited for their son to become of age, then took the veil in 1238 and became Abbess at Lacock. She probably founded Hinton Priory and Lacock Abbey on the same day in 1232.

Was the priory founded on a spirit path? Leys or spirit paths sometimes give rise to folk memories of 'tunnels' and there is a legend of a secret tunnel running from the priory ruins under the parish church and on to the George Inn, an ancient hostelry. The ghost of a young girl haunts this route as it goes through the grounds of Hinton House. The footpath between priory and church has been called Monks Way, as noted by Phil Quinn in *The Ley Hunter*, no. 128.

A Shakespearean connection

One of the monks, Brother Stephen at the end of the 15th century, was an ecstatic visionary. Nicholas Hopkins predicted that the third Duke of Buckingham would succeed to the throne. He found himself in the Tower for those words in 1521, while Buckingham was executed. Shakespeare's *Henry VIII* recorded the scene:

'*Surveyor:*   He was brought to this
          By a vain prophecy of Nicholas Hopkins.

King: What was that Hopkins?

Surveyor: Sir, a Chartreux friar,
          His confessor, who fed him every minute
          With words of sovereignty.'

The Walk

1. Face the Stag Inn from across the road and go right. Turn right along Branch Road for about half a mile, looking out for a public footpath signpost in the hedge on your left (ignore one that appears soon on your right).

2. Turn left to cross a stile beside the footpath signpost. Bear half-right through the field to another stile which is about 63 metres (70 yards) to the left of its far right corner. Go ahead, as waymarked, to pass shrubbery on your left and Hinton Priory (screened by a hedge) on your right. Continue over a stile beside a gate. Bear right to cross a stile beside a signpost and gate. Maintain this direction by cutting across the next field to a stile to the left of a gate halfway along a fence ahead.

3. Go ahead over the stile to walk through a field to another stile. Continue with a hedge on your left through two fields, go

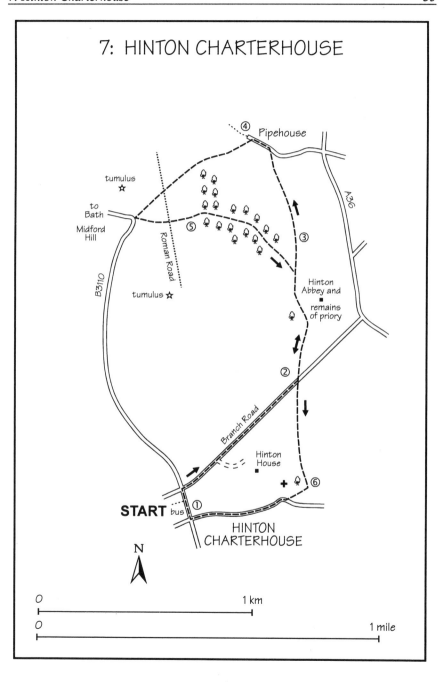

7: HINTON CHARTERHOUSE

④ Pipehouse

tumulus ☆

to Bath
Midford Hill

A36

⑤

③

Hinton Abbey and remains of priory

B3110

Roman Road

tumulus ☆

②

Branch Road

Hinton House

+ ⑥

START bus ①

HINTON CHARTERHOUSE

N

0	1 km

0	1 mile

ahead over more stiles to reach a narrow path leading straight ahead to a road. Go left to the end of this road and the last of the houses in Pipehouse.

4. Turn left over a stile and bear half-right to follow the way-marked path diagonally through a field. Go into its far right corner to take a stile shaded by trees. Maintain your direction through the next field (and over the course of a Roman road). Reach a stile giving access to a road at the top of Midford Hill, but don't go over it! Instead, turn sharply left to follow a fence on your right towards woodland.

5. Follow the path over a stile and through the woodland to emerge over a stile to the left of a gate at the end of an avenue of trees. Cross this to walk with a fence on your right. Return to the stile beside the signpost and gate in this fence and bear right over it to retrace your steps past Hinton Priory, now on your left, back to the road. Go ahead across the road carefully to follow the signposted path which leads to a patch of wood-land to the left of the church.

6. Cross a stile into the woodland and bear right through a kissing-gate to walk with a wall on your right towards the church of St John the Baptist. Pass this on your right to leave the churchyard by a metal kissing-gate on your left next to a public footpath signpost. Go right to follow the church's ac-cess drive to return to Hinton Charterhouse, where you turn right for the Stag Inn.

8. Cheddar

Route: Jacob's Ladder, Cheddar — West Mendip Way — Jacob's Ladder, Cheddar

Distance: 3 miles. Strenuous.

Maps: O.S. Explorer 4 Mendip Hills West; O.S. Landranger 182 Weston-super-Mare and Bridgwater.

Start: The foot of Jacob's Ladder, Cheddar (ST464539).

Access: Bus no. 126 runs to Cheddar from Weston-super-Mare and Wells (tel. 0117 955 3231).

Round and About

Jacob's Ladder

Cheddar Gorge, with its spectacular caves, is now a major tourist attraction. In the late 17th century it was a mining area, as the second chapter of E.W. Ryall's book *Second Time Round* records. This thought-provoking book describes the author's alleged previous life in 17th century Somerset and is said by some to be a case for reincarnation. In it, John Fletcher, as the author then was, made an expedition with his friend Jeremy Bragg to Jacob's Ladder. Tethering their horses at the foot of the cliff (where this walk starts), they climbed to see the magnificent view. Reaching the top, John suddenly felt the ground give way beneath him. He had fallen into a lead mine worked by Germans. He emerged one mile away from his horse and with a broken arm. Three hundred and one years later, in 1962, did John Fletcher's reincarnation really return to that spot?

Cheddar's deep limestone gorge is a dramatic sight, while the spectacular caves are not to be missed. Tests on the skeleton of a man dated to about 7000 BC and found in Gough's Cave in 1903 show that his DNA was very similar (though, admittedly, not identical) to that of a modern local schoolteacher so, despite invasions, the same people appear to have inhabited the Cheddar area for at least nine thousand years. This may not be an isolated instance, giving added credibility and longevity to folktales and legends. Perhaps the same souls have been reincarnating here for millennia too! Hopefully, they have advanced from the days when cannibalism was practised by cave-dwellers, as suggested by remains found here and displayed in the museum near Gough's Cave. The site of a royal palace dating from Saxon times was discovered in 1962 in the grounds of the local upper school. King Edmund would have been a resident on the day that his horse almost carried him over the edge of the gorge whilst out hunting in 941.

The Walk

1. A visit to the Cheddar Showcaves is highly recommended. Their ticket also gains you admission to Jacob's Ladder, whose steps can be climbed to start this walk.

An alternative start (using public roads and paths) is to face the entrance to Jacob's Ladder, go right to a road junction, turn left and fork left uphill. Turn left off this road and soon bear left up a public bridleway to pass the Lookout Tower and reach the top of Jacob's Ladder.

Whichever way you arrived, with your back to the top of Jacob's Ladder, go left to follow the waymarked Cheddar Showcaves Gorge Walk, keeping Cheddar Gorge on your left. Do not take a gate ahead. Continue with a fence on your right. Descend to a stile in it, go ahead over this and reach a junction with the waymarked West Mendip Way.

2. Turn sharply right to follow the West Mendip Way, as waymarked in the direction of Draycott. Reach a corner, where you ignore a gate in a wall on your left but continue over a stile in the corner. Go ahead to diverge slightly from the wall on your left, descend to meet a fence and walk with it on your left, then reach a dew pond on your right.

3. Go ahead and turn right along a path, ignoring a stile beside a gate in the corner on your left. Ignore a stile in the fence which you put on your left as you head down the path with Cheddar Reservoir ahead in the distance. Reach a waymarked path junction with the West Mendip Way. Let it go left as you go ahead to descend towards Cheddar.

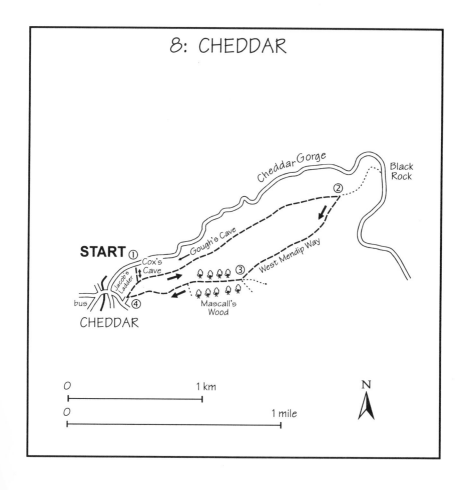

The view towards Cheddar Reservoir

4. Either turn right to follow the signposted public bridleway back to the top of Jacob's Ladder, where you can admire the views from the Lookout Tower before descending the steps, or bear left to join a road and turn right into Cheddar.

9. Wookey Hole

Route: Draycott – Priddy – Ebbor Gorge – Wookey Hole – Arthur's Point – Wells

Distance: 9½ miles. Strenuous. Linear route with bus stops at both ends.

Maps: O.S. Explorer 4 Mendip Hills West; O.S. Landranger 182 Weston-super-Mare and Bridgwater.

Start: Bus stop near the Red Lion Inn, Draycott (ST477514).

Finish: Bus station, Wells (ST546454).

Access: Bus no. 126 (Weston-super-Mare to Wells) connects the two ends of this linear walk. There is also a bus stop in Wookey Hole for the 172 service to Wells (tel. 0117 9553231 for details).

Round and About

Wells Cathedral

This linear walk finishes at Wells Cathedral, famed as one of the largest in Europe and with a hugely impressive West Front (see photograph). Nearby Vicars' Close, originally built by Bishop Ralph of Shrewsbury in the fourteenth century is the oldest continuously inhabited street in Europe.

The nearby Cathedral School was founded in the twelfth century to provide education for a handful of choir boys. Today, the School has over 800 girls and boys and enjoys a reputation for high academic standards together with a tradition of musical excellence.

The Witch of Wookey

Visit the Great Cave of Wookey Hole (open daily, admission fee) to see the figure of a witch who was turned to stone. As the once-beautiful witch lost her own charms, through practising the black arts, she became jealous of the happy young lovers that chanced upon her abode. She conjured up evil spirits to destroy one couple's relationship, leaving the young man heartbroken. He became a monk at Glastonbury Abbey and in time, when the locals requested the help of the Abbot of Glastonbury, he volunteered to confront the witch in her cave, armed with just a cross and a phial of holy water. In the face of her spells, the monk prayed and splashed the holy water over her, turning the witch to stone.

In 1912 a female skeleton dating from Arthurian times was found in Wookey Hole, with a witch-ball beside it. This may give substance to the story of Culhwch and Owen in *The Mabinogion*, where the legendary King Arthur is said to have slain a black witch who lived at 'the head of the Valley of Grief in the uplands of Hell'.

Poetic inspiration

Coleridge visited Wookey Hole before penning the lines:

> *'Where Alph, the sacred river, ran,*
> *Through caverns measureless to man'.*

The River Axe flows through Wookey Hole. The Druids saw this as the divine river of life emerging from the womb of the Earth-Mother-Goddess. The Axe corresponds to the Styx, where Charon's boat ferries souls of the dead to the Otherworld (the Celtic Annwn).

The waters draining into the Axe come from Priddy, meaning 'earth' in the sense of a world that is part of a cosmic system, 'As Above, So Below'. Pryderi was a lord of Annwn, while the legendary Arthur's ship was Prydwen.

A local saying is 'As sure as the Lord was at Priddy', referring to the local legend that the young Jesus came here with his great-uncle Joseph of Arimathea, the tin-trader. Was William Blake right to ponder:

> *'And did those feet in ancient time*
> *Walk upon England's mountains green,*
> *And was the Holy Lamb of God*
> *On England's pleasant pastures seen'?*

The Walk

1. Face the Red Lion Inn, go right, reach Draycott's Card Memorial and turn left up a lane waymarked as being the West Mendip Way (in the direction of Priddy). This steep lane deteriorates to become a grassy, hedged, track. Climb with this to a gate, go ahead beside a hedge, succeeded by a wall, on your right. Cross a stone stile in the corner ahead. Go ahead to cross a stone stile in a fence just to the left of a hedge ahead. Continue to cross a stile to the right of a gate in the next wall ahead. Converge with a wall on your right, on the other side of which was an Iron Age settlement. Pass a patch of woodland on your right.

2. Go ahead over the stone stile in the corner, maintain your direction to continue over a waymarked stone stile in the wall ahead, about 90 metres (100 yards) to the left of a small group of trees. Walk parallel with a wall 45 metres (50 yards) away on your right in the next field and cross a stile in a wall ahead. Go ahead through the next field, cross a stile and continue to the far right-hand corner of the following field. Proceed beside a wall on your right in a field which brings you to a road at a junction.

3. Crossing a road, go ahead along the road opposite. Bear right with the waymarked West Mendip Way to take a stone stile and cross a stile in the wall ahead as you aim for the left-hand corner of the next field to join a road. Go right along this into Priddy, ignoring a turning immediately on your left. Pass the New Inn on your right and fork right to pass the Queen Victoria Inn on your right.

4. Turn left over a stile to follow the West Mendip Way, as waymarked for Wookey Hole. Continue around the left-hand edge of this field to cross a stile in its far right-hand corner. Continue beside a wall on your left, turn left to take a stile in it, immediately turn right and walk along an enclosed path.

5. Emerge over a stile and turn left along a green lane, Dursdon Drove. Pass another track on your left, go ahead 45 metres (50 yards) then turn right along a track to Higher Pitts Farm. Follow the waymarked path between the farmhouses, continue through a small metal gate and go right to walk with a hedge on your right. Cross a stile beside a gate in the corner ahead and bear right with a fence on your right and a fine view over Glastonbury Tor on your left. Take a stile to the left of a gate in the corner to enter Ebbor Gorge National Nature Reserve. Continue downhill and bearing left. Go straight ahead at a junction in the woodland. Turn left at the bottom of a steeply descending path with steps. Continue to reach a road.

6. Go left along the road to pass the entrance to the famous caves of Wookey Hole on your left. Pass Milton Lane on your left and soon bear left with the West Mendip Way through a kissing-gate. Climb with a hedge on your right. Take a kissing-gate in the corner, follow an enclosed path and reach another kissing-gate. Go through this and bear left with the waymarked West Mendip Way to climb past woodland on your left up Arthur's Point, said to have been used as a look-out point by King Arthur. Turn sharply right to descend through woodland, go over a stile and bear left to take a gate in the corner. Avoid a dangerous lane ahead by following the waymarked West Mendip Way through woodland. Follow this to bear left, then emerge from the wood in the bottom right-hand corner, where a waymark post directs you to go right, along a track.

7. Go ahead at a track junction and reach a waymark post at what is now a lane junction. Do not go ahead at the danger sign (the lane is liable to subsidence because of the old quarry to your right). Turn left over a stile in a hedge, turn right immediately to follow the hedge on your right. Turn right across another stile and go left along what is now a safe lane. When the lane bears left, go straight ahead with the waymarked footpath. De-

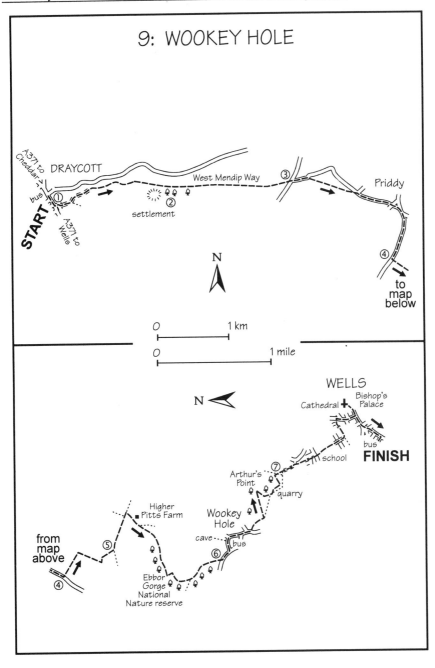

9: WOOKEY HOLE

scend with a narrow path, cross a road, emerge on a lower road and turn left for nine metres (10 yards) before turning right down the signposted public footpath which goes through the grounds of a school and across a new road by a footbridge. Go left along Lovers' Walk and bear right in a corner to take a passage to emerge on New Street. Go right to pass the West Front of Wells Cathedral on your left. Follow Sadler Street to reach the Market Place, where you can divert left to visit the cathedral, the bishop's palace and its bell-ringing swans. Continue along the High Street and Broad Street to reach Wells bus station on your right.

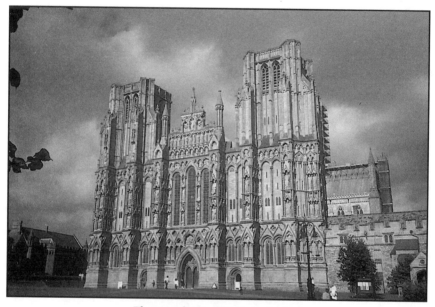

The west front of Wells Cathedral

10. Doone Country

Route: County Gate—Malmsmead—Cloud Farm—Extension into Devon to visit Lank Combe and Hoccombe—Cloud Farm—Oare—Yenworthy—County Gate

Distance: 10 miles (of which 4 are in Somerset, 6 in Devon). Strenuous

Maps: O.S. Outdoor Leisure 9 Exmoor; O.S. Landranger 180 Barnstaple and Ilfracombe plus 181 Minehead and Brendon Hills.

Start: County Gate (SS794486).

Access: Bus no. 300 runs to County Gate from Bridgwater or Taunton, Minehead and Ilfracombe (tel. 01823 272033).

Round and About

Who were the Doones?

When R.D. Blackmore penned *Lorna Doone* (first published in 1869), he was writing much more than a novel. Fact is stranger than fiction and it is fascinating to discover the true history which the novelist felt compelled to obscure a little. This famous romance of Exmoor is set on the border of Somerset and Devon. The outlaw Doones paid little heed to county boundaries, except to find them convenient when the Authorities could be tempted into pushing their problem onto their neighbours rather than dealing with it. So, this walk begins and ends in Somerset, but in our pursuit of literary heroes and villains an excursion is made into Devon, even along moorland paths not blessed with official status. Please treat these Devonian miles as an extra in the manner of the baker's dozen. The right of way on the Devon side of Badgworthy Water may be labelled as leading to Doone Country on the OS Outdoor Leisure map, but the real Doone Country is actually up Lank Combe. Sir Atholl Oakeley's booklet *The Facts on which Blackmore based Lorna Doone* and the excellent booklet *Who was Lorna Doone?* by Barry Gardner make this clear.

Blackmore set his story in the 17th century. A Scottish nobleman, Sir Ensor Doone, had been forced to seek refuge on Exmoor around 1640. In desperation and with a sense of seeking revenge on society, his family and retainers became bandits terrorising the region and gaining wives by abducting the daughters of local farmers. In the novel, Lorna, the daughter of the Doones' number-one foe from Scotland, Lord Dugal, was kidnapped in 1673, given the Doone name and brought up to marry Carver Doone, Sir Ensor's successor. This would bring Lorna's title and inheritance to Carver.

A hero arrives in the shape of John Ridd. Falling in love with young Lorna, whom he met by chance on St Valentine's Day, 1675, he rescues her. The yeoman then has to endure his love being summoned to Court as Lady Dugal. She does return to marry John in Oare Church; however, as she stands at the altar Carver Doone shoots her. All ends happily when the villain sinks into a bog and Lorna is found to have been wounded, not killed.

Blackmore could have based his story on records kept by his grandfather, the rector of Oare and Combe Martin. Like John Ridd, he had gone to Blundell's School, Tiverton. The Blackmores had lived in the area as long as the Doones and the novelist pointed towards his detailed knowledge of the origin of the Doones when he named his wise-woman Mother Melldrum. This can be taken as a reference to Meldrum, Aberdeenshire, where the Gordon Earls of Huntly were descended from King Dugal of Lorne.

Blackmore chose to write as if events happened 20 years later than they actually did, making 1653 become 1673, for instance. This gave his novel the flavour of the Monmouth Uprising of 1685, which can be taken as an embellishment to the story. The real Lorna was born in 1645, not 1665. This would make her a contemporary of the real 'Girt' John Ridd, a famous Exmoor wrestler.

Sir James Stewart unfairly lost his vast Scottish estates and title in 1607. Falling in with outlaws, he became known by the Gaelic name Iain Ciar Duine (chosen dusky man). Forced to leave Scotland, he settled with his clan in a remote Exmoor valley, probably in 1623. The locals recognised him as a knight and their pronunciation of his name turned it into 'Sir Ensor Doone'. Still seeking a return to their noble status, the Doones kidnapped the infant Lorna, whose birth in 1645 had hastened the secret marriage of Lady Mary Grant of Freuchie and Lewis Gordon of Huntly in late 1644. This wedding united two hostile clans and made Lorna the heir to a vast fortune and estates. So, the girl was brought up in Lank Combe until the day John Ridd rescued her.

This walk begins by overlooking Malmsmead, where Blackmore's Churchwarden Nicholas Snowe lived at what is now

Doone country: starting to walk up Lank Combe

Lorna Doone Farm. Records do show that a Snow daughter was married from here in 1699. The first footbridge is over the Oare Water, called the Lynn Stream in *Lorna Doone*. John Ridd used to go fishing here. It was John's search for roaches that led him up Badgworthy Water (Blackmore's Bagworthy Water), past where a memorial stone to the novelist was placed in 1969, then, turning right, up Lank Combe. This is the real Doone Valley, where the outlaws lived in wooden huts (to be destroyed by fire), in a valley 'carved from the Mountains in a perfect oval'. The famous waterslide is near the footbridge and confluence.

The ruins above where Hoccombe Water and Badgworthy Water mingle date back to the 11th century. They housed the Brethren of St John of Jerusalem. The Doones settled elsewhere, although Lorna Doone (a Roman Catholic) is said to have been buried here, some three miles westward of the Wizard's Slough that engulfed Carver Doone.

The church of St Mary the Virgin, Oare, is where Lorna was shot by Carver Doone as she married John Ridd. A film showed Carver shooting through a side window, but the shot could have come from the open west end of the church. The western tower and the eastern chancel are 19th century additions, so the altar steps where Lorna fell would have been west of the present screen. This shooting incident in the church is one part of the story that Blackmore may have borrowed from elsewhere for dramatic effect, anyway. The novelist was probably inspired by the story of Mary Whyddon, who was shot by a jealous lover as she entered The Three Crowns Hotel, Chagford (Dartmoor) after her wedding in nearby St Michael's church in 1641.

Oare House, near the path from the church up to the A39, was the site of John Ridd's Plover's Barrows Farm. It provides a direct 'gun-barrel' view of the churchyard. As you approach Yenworthy, recall how Blackmore told of Widow Fisher firing a great long-gun at the Doones when they threatened to rob her house. She so gained the respect of the outlaws that they said, 'She ought to be a Doone!'

Not far away, just above Embelle Woods at about grid ref. SS810490 may lie the lost and secret graves of the Doones (cf *Secret Exmoor* by Peter Hesp). Below, on Glenthorne Beach (SS805495), is one of the places where the young Jesus is said to have landed with his tin-trading Great-Uncle Joseph of Arimathea.

The Walk

1. With your back to and on the same side of the road as the walkers' shelter, bear right to take the signposted bridleway for Doone Valley, Oare and Malmsmead. Take a gate and descend with a fence on your left. When this comes to an end, ignore a gate in the corner and bear right downhill to take a footbridge over Oare Water and reach a road.

2. Go right for 180 metres (200 yards), then turn left along the access lane to Cloud Farm, where refreshments are available.

3. Extend this walk into Devon, if you wish, by turning right over a footbridge across Badgworthy Water. Go left to walk with the river on your left, going upstream. Pass the memorial stone to R.D. Blackmore on your right. After one mile, it is possible to bear right with a woodland path and emerge in Lank Coombe. A clear path climbs the right-hand side of this genuine Doone Valley. After taking a gate, it is possible to descend near a fence on your left to join the stream and go right upstream to the path junction at Lankcombe Ford.

4. Return to Badgworthy Water by turning around to walk downstream with the stream on your right. Pass the Waterslide as you come to woodland and approach a footbridge. Turn right to cross this and resume walking with Badgworthy Water on your left, going upstream to the next confluence. This is with Hoccombe Water, above which are the ruins of the 11th-century religious settlement.

5. Return to Cloud Farm by turning around and walking downstream with Badgworthy Water on your right. Turn right to cross the footbridge again back to Cloud Farm, where refreshments are available.

6. Back in Somerset, pass Cloud Farm's access lane on your left, but do bear left with the signposted footpath for Oare Church.

This climbs uphill, takes two gates, keeps a hedge on your left and bears right to continue through a waymarked gate and past sheep-pens. Bear slightly right in the next field to take a gate ahead and go left past a wooded ravine on your left. Follow the waymarked bridleway (blue arrows) through a gate and downhill to a road.

7. Turn left to pass Oare Church on your left. Turn right to take a road across Oare Water and ignore a signposted public footpath on your right immediately after this. Pass the entrance to Oare House on your right and immediately after this, turn right along the signposted public footpath to Yenworthy. This takes a stile and climbs through a patch of woodland above the house on your right, then descends to cross a stile in a fence on your right. Turn left up a track. Go ahead over a stile to the left of a gate across the track and pass gorse on your left. Ignore a path turning left uphill. Go ahead with the path waymarked with yellow paint to walk with a fence on your right. Climb to the A39 road, cross it carefully and take the access lane for Yenworthy ahead. Fork right to pass Yenworthy Lodge on your left.

8. When the trees shielding Yenworthy Lodge end, turn left to take a track that soon bears right, then goes left through moorland. There is a view over the sea on your right. Go ahead to return to the bus stop, walkers' shelter and National Park Visitors' Centre at County Gate.

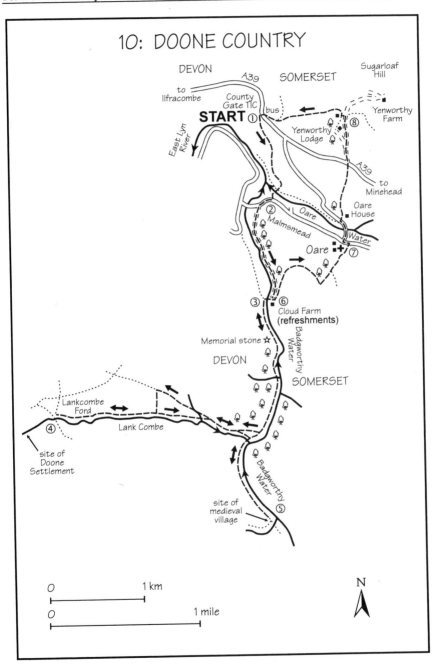

10: DOONE COUNTRY

11. Porlock

Route: Stone Circle – Hawkcombe Head – Porlock

Distance: 4½ miles (linear route between bus stops). Easy.

Maps: O.S. Outdoor Leisure 9 Exmoor; O.S. Landranger 181 Minehead and Brendon Hills.

Start: Stone circle near sheep fold, unmarked request bus stop for service no. 285 (SS845446).

Finish: Porlock Library bus stop (SS888468).

Access: Take the North Exmoor Visitor Bus (no. 285, tel. 01823 358232). Buy a circular ticket (Minehead-Exford-Porlock-Minehead) allowing you to alight at the start and board at the finish. Bus no. 300 (Taunton or Bridgwater, Minehead-Ilfracombe) serves both Porlock and Whitstone Post, on the A39 north of Hawicombe Head, while bus no. 38 runs to Porlock from Minehead (tel. 01823 272033).

Round and About

Murder most foul

Exmoor bears many traces of our prehistoric ancestors, as described by Hazel Eardley-Wilmot in her book *Ancient Exmoor*. This walk starts from a good example of a stone circle, south of the old flintknapping site at Hawkcombe Head. My dowsing revealed the most important ley or spirit path running through it to be aligned with sunrise and sunset at the equinoxes.

Jack Hurley's book *Murder and Mystery on Exmoor* describes a tragic murder in Parson's Street, Porlock, on 3 June, 1914. Henry Quartly, aged 55, shot his neighbour Henry Pugsley, aged 59, then was foiled in an attempt to shoot himself by the bravery of the village policeman, Joseph Greedy. Pleading guilty, Quartly was hanged at Shepton Mallet on 10 November, 1914.

Lifeboat Heroism

Porlock was the destination of the Lynmouth lifeboat on 12 January, 1899. A force-eight gale suddenly blew up in the early afternoon and the lifeboat was called out to help a boat in distress in Porlock Bay. Unable to launch the lifeboat in Lynmouth, the crew took the lifeboat overland the 15 miles to Porlock overnight, losing a wheel off the undercarriage when halfway up Countisbury. Later the undercarriage proved too wide for the road and had to be taken across Exmoor for two miles. A cottage garden wall was knocked down before Porlock was reached just before dawn. With the aid of a tug, they still managed to rescue their target, the *Forest Hall*, but had to land at Barry in South Wales. As the heroes said when recounting the story of their rescue, 'It was impossible ... so it took a bit longer'.

The Walk

1. Alight from the no. 285 North Exmoor Visitor Bus – **on request** – some five miles north of Exford and one mile north of Lucott Cross, where there is a sheep fold on your left (going north) immediately after the road crosses a stream. A gate on your left gives access to the field containing the sheep fold and above this is a stone circle. Returning to the road, go north, passing the stone circle behind the hedge on your left. Climb gradually to where a signposted bridleway forks left ahead. Bear right with the road for 180 metres

Porlock stone circle

(200 yards), pass under power lines and reach the path junction at Hawkcombe Head.

2. Turn right down a signposted bridleway to Porlock. Keep the stream on your right as you walk down the valley and follow the path through woodland.

3. Go ahead across a ford, continue through a gate and cross a second ford to resume walking with the stream on your right. Go ahead along the bridleway signposted for Hawk Combe at a signposted path junction. Keep to the lower path, near the stream on your right. Take a footbridge to continue with the stream on your left, then cross a second footbridge to resume walking with the stream on your right.

4. Emerge on a roughly-metalled lane and bear right with this, keeping the stream on your right. Ignore a signposted bridleway when it forks right. Follow the lane, which is soon joined by another lane coming sharply from your right. Go ahead down Parson's Street, with the stream changing to your left-hand side, to reach St Dubricius' Church (this was the St Dyfrig who was said to have crowned King Arthur, probably in AD 497 at Woodchester in Gloucestershire), Porlock, on your right. Go right along Porlock's High Street for the bus stops.

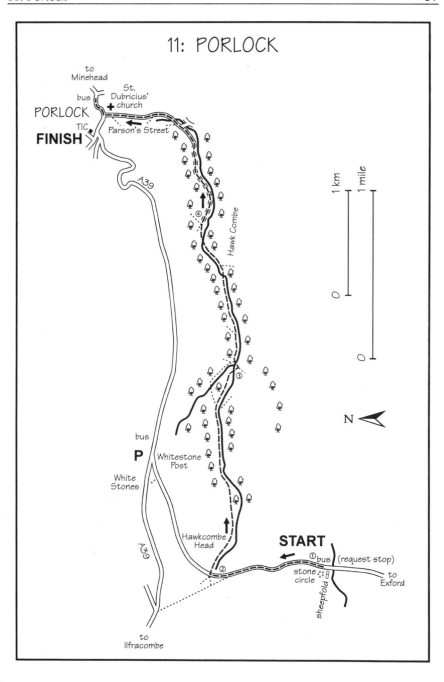

11: PORLOCK

to Minehead

bus

PORLOCK

St. Dubricius' church

TIC

FINISH

Parson's Street

A39

Hawk Combe

④

1 km

1 mile

0

0

N

bus

P

Whitestone Post

White Stones

③

Hawkcombe Head

START

bus (request stop)

①

②

stone circle

sheepfold

to Exford

A39

to Ilfracombe

to Minehead

12. Dunster Castle

Route: Carhampton – Dunster – Gallox Bridge – Carhampton

Distance: 4¼ miles. Easy.

Maps: O.S. Outdoor Leisure 9 Exmoor; O.S. Landranger 181 Minehead and Brendon Hills.

Start: Carhampton bus stop (ST007427)

Access: Buses nos. 15 (Bridgwater-Minehead), 28 (Minehead-Taunton), 300 (Taunton-Ilfracombe) and 305 (Minhead-Williton) serve Carhampton. Tel. 01823 358232 for details.

Round and About

A Vegan Dragon

Dunster is known as a medieval village and the twin breasts of hills overlooking it are occupied by a castle (now in the care of the National Trust) bought by the Luttrel family for 5000 marks (£3333) in 1376 and an 18th century folly (Conyger Tower). Both would seem to be the focus of leys, spirit paths or 'dragon energy lines'.

In the early sixth century, when the legendary King Arthur ruled this part of Somerset in alliance with Cadwy, a local chieftain, there was said to be a real live dragon breathing fire in the marshes on the seaward side. It carried off humans as well as animals, so when St Carantoc (the Welsh St Carannog, son or grandson of Ceredig, whose name lives on in Llangrannog in Ceredigion) floated here from Wales on his marvellous marble altar, Arthur asked the saint to deal with it. Anybody able to float on a marble altar must have miraculous powers so, after prayers and incantations, the dragon rose up out of the bog and devotedly bowed its head as if waiting to be blessed at the altar rail! St Carantoc led it up to the court at Dunster Castle before releasing it back in the marshes which border Kitrow Lane, followed near the start of this walk. The dragon had meekly promised never to harm anyone again and never to eat animal food – it became a vegan! St Carantoc is said to have built the first church at Carhampton.

The Walk

1. With your back to the bus shelter, use the pelican crossing to reach the other side of the A39 road (if you aren't there already) and go right. Reach the Butcher's Arms pub on your right and bear left down a No Through Road, passing St John the Baptist's Church on your right. Go ahead along a grassy, hedged, track, signposted as the public footpath to Blue Anchor Bay. Keep to this hedged track (Kitrow Lane) ignoring two stiles on your right.

2. Bear right at the track junction and almost immediately ignore a turning (Saltry Lane) on your right. Bear left to the A39 and cross this road carefully to turn right along its cycle path for half a mile. Dunster Castle can be seen on your left and Conyger Tower crowns another conical hill ahead.

3. Cross Loxhole Bridge and bear left to take a kissing-gate and follow the signposted public footpath to Dunster. This goes across the drive to Dunster Castle and through parkland. Walk with the fence of a car park on your right and bear right through a small wooden gate in the corner to reach a road (Dunster Steep). Go left to pass Dunster Visitor Centre on your left. Bear left along the High Street. Do not turn right into Church Street. Go ahead up the hill, turn right and pass the entrance to Dunster Castle on your left. Continue downhill towards West Street. There is a display of model houses near the Teddy Bear shop on the corner. Bear, appropriately, left down West Street.

4. Turn left along Mill Lane. Reach a junction where you will turn right, as signposted for the packhorse bridge. Divert ahead if you wish to visit the working watermill first. Going right towards the packhorse bridge (Gallox Bridge), pass a car park on your left and bear left. Cross the packhorse bridge and go ahead with a fence on your left to reach a signposted path junction.

Gallox Bridge

5. Turn left to take a bridleway signposted for Carhampton and Withycombe. Cross a stile and immediately ignore a signposted bridleway forking right to Withycombe. Go ahead along the signposted footpath for Carhampton. Pass woodland away to your right, walk near a fence on your left and go ahead through a small wooden gate to the right of a field gate ahead to continue near a hedge on your left in the next field.

6. Turn left down a hedged track signposted as a public path to Carhampton. This soon becomes a metalled lane. Pass a signposted path on your left, then a lane on your right. Pass Winsors Lane on your left. Go ahead along Parke Lane. Turn left along the High Street to return to the bus stop in Carhampton.

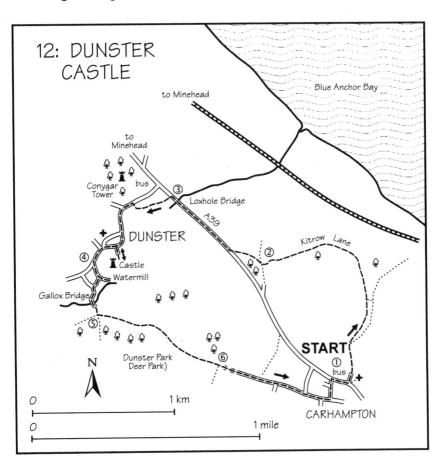

12: DUNSTER CASTLE

to Minehead

Blue Anchor Bay

to Minehead

Conygar Tower   bus   ③   Loxhole Bridge

A39

DUNSTER   Kitrow Lane

④   ②

Castle
Watermill

Gallox Bridge

⑤

⑥   **START** ①

N

Dunster Park
Deer Park)   bus

0   1 km

0   1 mile

CARHAMPTON

13. Shervage Wood

Route: Holford – Woodlands Hill – Walford's Gibbet – Castle of Comfort – Shervage Wood – Woodlands Hill – Holford

Distance: 5¼ miles. Strenuous.

Maps: O.S. Explorer 22 Quantock Hills and Bridgwater; O.S. Landranger 181 Minehead and Brendon Hills.

Start: The Plough Inn, Holford (ST158413).

Access: Bus no. 15 (Bridgwater-Minehead) serves Holford (tel. 01823 272033).

Round and About

The Ghost of a Hanged Man

Walford's Gibbet has earned its name on the modern Ordnance Survey map. It is a reminder of a gruesome deed in 1789. John Walford was a handsome 24-year old charcoal-burner, well-liked in his birthplace of Over Stowey. The miller's daughter, Ann Rice, was understood to harbour love for him, but perhaps John's poverty discouraged marriage. Lonely in his simple shelter on the hills, John was visited by an unattractive girl called Jenny. He made her pregnant and the parish overseers put pressure on him; when Jenny produced a second child, John was arrested and forced to marry her. The weddinq took place on 18 June, 1789. On 5 July, 1789, John lost his temper with his wife and killed her. A drinking trip to the Castle of Comfort pub was involved in the story. Many friends testified as to John's good character at his trial in Bridgwater that 18 August. Hanged on 20 August, Ann Rice climbed into the cart for his last ride to the gallow trees. John's handsome body was suspended in an iron cage for a year and a day, then buried under the gallows tree. His ghost still haunts the spot.

A Great Worm?

Enter Shervage Wood at your peril. A 'Gurt Vurm', or dragon, lived here. By day it would coil itself around trees. It lived off human flesh, as well as sheep and cattle, so it was a great relief when a woodman came from Stogumber and cut it in two with his axe.

The path on Woodlands Hill, Holford

The Walk

1. With a garage on your left and the Plough Inn on your right, walk away from the A39 road by bearing sharply left through the village of Holford. Pass the lych-gate for St Mary's Church on your left, go left at a road junction and soon keep left when the road forks. Reach a small triangle of grass and turn sharply left uphill, with woodland at first on your right. This lane gradually descends to join the A39.

2. As you approach the A39, turn right to follow a bridleway signposted for Crowcombe. Take a gate to enter the National

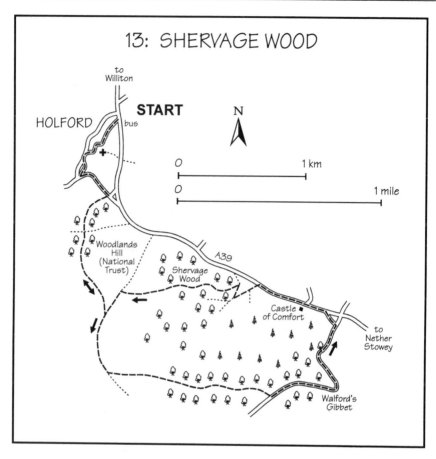

13: SHERVAGE WOOD

to
Williton

START

N

HOLFORD bus

O ————————— 1 km

O ————————————— 1 mile

Woodlands
Hill
(National
Trust)

A39

Shervage
Wood

Castle
of Comfort

to
Nether
Stowey

Walford's
Gibbet

Trust's Woodlands Hill. Go ahead to climb gradually through woodland, passing a small wooden gate on your right. Emerge at the edge of heather moorland and take the main path ahead. Follow this over the brow of the hill, going south.

3. Turn left at a path junction to walk east along a permissive path which keeps below the hillfort crowning the summit on your right. Go ahead to follow this path through woodland and emerge on a lane.

4. Go left downhill and pass the site of Walford's Gibbet on your

left as the lane emerges from the woods and turns sharply left. Continue downhill to the A39.

5. Cross the A39 to turn left and walk along it carefully for half a mile, passing the Castle of Comfort pub on your left.

6. Bear left over a stile beside a gate to enter Shervage Wood. Go ahead 360 metres (400 yards) to a path junction and turn sharply right to climb a slope. Turn sharply left at a higher path junction and follow this path through Shervage Wood (beware of dragons!). Emerge on moorland and go ahead to join a clear path which you turn left along. Climb to a. junction with another path. Turn right to retrace your steps back to Holford.

14. Glastonbury

Route: Abbey ruins—Wearyall Hill—Chalice Well—Tor—Dod Lane—Abbey ruins

Distance: 3½ miles. Strenuous.

Maps: O.S. Explorer 4 (141) Mendip Hills West; O.S. Landrangers 182 (Weston-super-Mare & Bridgwater) or 183 (Yeovil & Frome).

Start: Entrance to abbey ruins, Glastonbury (ST 499388).

Access: Buses to Glastonbury include no. 376 (Bristol-Yeovil), tel. 01823 358299.

Around and About

Glastonbury and its Zodiac

Glastonbury has the strongest mystical and sacred connections of any town in Britain, as can easily be confirmed by walking down its streets and observing the plethora of shops selling crystals, candles, joss sticks and other New Age paraphernalia. Its greatest claim to fame however, is its famous tor, which has long been linked with early Christian history and traditions of magic, myth, legends and leylines. Certainly, Glastonbury Tor is both an extraordinary landmark with amazing views and is felt by many to be a sacred site with unique qualities.

The other remarkable aspect of this area is The Glastonbury Zodiac (also known as The Glastonbury Giants). This is a huge circular feature of the landscape measuring 10 miles across. Local legends and place names had, for hundreds of years, associated topological aspects of the surrounding countryside with human or animal forms. Katherine Maltwood, in the 1930s, went further by inventing (or rediscovering) the Zodiac, claiming that along its circumference one can discern the 12 signs of the zodiac in the shapes of hills, valleys, rivers and so on, distributed around the mystical 'Isle of Avalon'. Adherents claim that the sign of Aries is to be found at Street and, significantly for this walk, that the Phoenix of Aquarius rises from Glastonbury Tor. Some also believe that the Zodiac represents King Arthur's Round Table, with the main characters seated around it.

The Sign of Aquarius

Several years ago, Mary Caine, whose words form the preface of this book, was making a film about the Zodiac's giant landscape figures. She and her husband decided to sleep at the foot of the Tor in their dormobile. They eventually gained permission to park in a field from a farmer who arrived carrying water for his cows in milk churns. This, they attributed as a sign from Aquarius, the water carrier. It is of interest that, in the Zodiac, Aquarius is signed by a great Phoenix, the mythical bird who dies in old age and renews himself by self-immolation on a nest of spices (Ashwell Lane and Cinnamon Lane on this effigy thus becoming curiously significant). The Tor represents the head of the phoenix, while Chalice Well is said to be its beak.

It is claimed that Chalice Well is where Joseph of Arimathea (a title borne by James the brother of Jesus after the crucifixion, according to *Bloodline of the Holy Grail* by Laurence Gardner) hid the cup used at the Last Supper and in which was collected Jesus' blood, tears and sweat at the crucifixion (stored in two cruets). The cup isn't there now (and wasn't there in the Middle Ages to be exploited by the monks), having been carried westwards for safety from the Saxon menace in the sixth century, after the Battle of Camlan. Three Arthurian knights (the three guardians of the Grail who achieved its Quest, being Galahad, who has been identified as the historical Cadoc, Perceval the historical Pedrog, and Derfel, a pupil of the aged Bors) were given it by St Bridget. They carried it into Ceredigion (now in Wales) and the chalice is now known as the Nanteos Cup.

Ley lines around Glastonbury

The Dragon Line described by John Michell in *The New View Over*

Atlantis and followed in detail by Hamish Miller and Paul Broadhurst in *The Sun and the Serpent* forms the axis line of the Tor. At an angle of 63 degrees, it is aligned with sunrise at Beltane (May lst) and Lughnasadh (August lst). Two stones on the western side of the Tor mark it out. The lower stone is known as the Living Rock. It continues through the ruined tower of what was a church dedicated to St Michael at the 512ft summit. Hamish Miller dowsed the female 'Mary' energy forming a container (chalice) on the Tor which is penetrated by the male 'Michael' energy in a demonstration of alchemical fusion.

A similar pattern of lines is visible spiralling around the Tor as a three-dimensional labyrinth, as Geoffrey Ashe has written about in *The Glastonbury Tor Maze*. The Living Rock marks its entrance, where the Quest Knight can start along the path of trial, error and suffering in the hope of achieving the Grail, taking the 'seven planetary steps to perfection'. Like Perceval, he can 'pierce the vale' by having (like the phoenix) re-made himself, 'Par Luit Fait'. Here is the Glass Mountain of self-analysis that is so difficult to climb, yet so easy to slide down.

Christian, Celtic and other connections

The Tor can be likened to a pyramid – the 'pyre amid' our burning phoenix. Like Sinai, a Mount of Transfiguration, this is a place for visions and prophecies, inspiration and rejuvenation. Lives are altered here, given new purposes and places in the world. The conscious mind can be joined with the universal subconscious. Here is the Jerusalem of William Blake. Stephen Jenkins, author of *The Undiscovered Country* equates Glastonbury with Shambhala – did St Collen encounter Gwyn ap Nudd, Lord of Annwn, the Celtic Otherworld, on the Tor?

Glastonbury Abbey lies between the signs of Pisces and Aquarius on the famous Zodiac. Wearyall Hill is shaped like a fish and this is where it is claimed that Joseph of Arimathea, after landing at the Gog and Magog oak trees, came with his weary band, planting his staff here. A cutting said to have been taken from it still flowers every January 4th (Christmas Eve by the old calendar). This Holy Thorn hails from the Holy Land and now adorns the Celtic Salmon of Wisdom.

When Bligh Bond excavated in the abbey, inspired by psychic messages, as he recorded in *The Gate of Remembrance*, an egg stone or Omphalos was found. It can be found behind the Abbot's Kitchen. Here, according to Kathy Jones in *The Goddess of Glastonbury*, sat the menstruating Oracle. Harmony and balance between the sexes is the true state for such a sacred spot, creating a unified fusion. As that great Glastonbury geomancer Anthony Roberts wrote (in issue 4, Spring 1984, of *Earth Giant*), 'at Glastonbury there is the marriage of Heaven and Earth'.

Glastonbury is also the location of the legendary 'Twelve Hides' – the area of land said to have been granted by the British King Arviragus to Joseph of Arimathea after the crucifixion. Some say that the first wattle and daub church was built here before then by Jesus' own hands when on a visit to Somerset in his youth with his tin-trading great-uncle. In support of this, there have been recent claims that Jesus was trained as an architect. The brand of Christianity espoused here describes Jesus as a Prophet, rather than as the Son of God. This indicates its direct source, unlike the later dogma imposed by the Vatican after politicians and power-seekers corrupted the original message of Jesus at Councils such as Nicaea in 325.

The tower of St Michael's Chapel, Glastonbury Tor

King Arviragus is most probably buried in the abbey today. He is reputed to have been the Arthur whose grave was dug up by the monks in 1191, probably to help raise funds after the fire of 1184. The famous sixtb-century King Arthur of Gwent is not, however, buried here. The mistaken identity is understandable, while the oak coffin suggests a first century burial. The cross that was found need not have been a forgery, although its Latin inscription compares with those of the 10th century rather than the sixth – it was probably placed there then. The tomb was originally about 50 feet (15m) from the south door of the abbey's Lady Chapel and is now marked as being in front of the abbey's High Altar. This places it on a ley or spirit path which goes eastwards along Dod Lane (a significant name) to Stonehenge. Many other such lines converge on Glastonbury and some are featured in other walks of this book (such as at Cadbury Castle).

The Walk

1. With your back to the abbey entrance, go left along Magdalene Street. Turn right along Street Road and when the houses on your left come to an end, bear left through a kissing-gate in the hedge to climb Wearyall Hill to a thorn tree on its ridge.

2. Walk back along the ridge of Wearyall Hill to a stile giving access to a road on your right (Hillhead). Continue along this and go ahead with Bere Lane to pass the Rural Life Museum on your right. Bear right along Chilkwell Street to reach Chalice Well on your left.

3. Turn left along Wellhouse Lane and immediately turn right to take the footpath which climbs to the top of Glastonbury Tor. Follow this path as it descends and bears left to a road.

4. Go left along the road to pass the Tor on your left. Ignore a road turning on your right. Do bear right over a stile to climb up a

field to a stile giving access to an enclosed path. Follow this to a road and go ahead (left) along this.

5. Take a kissing-gate in the corner ahead when the road turns left. Go ahead down the left-hand side of pasture which slopes downhill on your right. Continue down Dod Lane and emerge on Chilkwell Street, where you go right.

6. Turn left to follow Silver Street and bear right at its end to reach the High Street. Go left and turn left back to the abbey entrance.

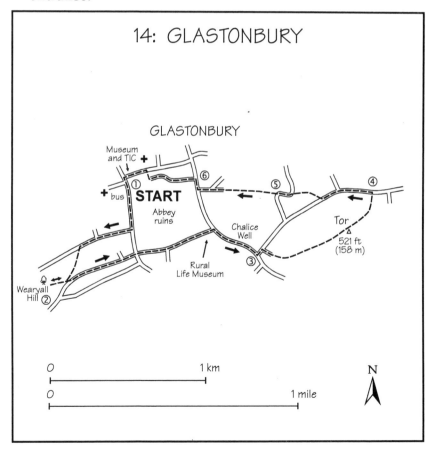

15. The Caratacus Stone

Route: Winsford — Caratacus Stone — The Punchbowl — Winsford

Distance: 5½ miles. Strenuous.

Maps: O.S. Outdoor Leisure 9 Exmoor; O.S. Landranger 181 Minehead and Brendon Hills.

Start: Winsford Memorial (SS906349).

Access: Bus no. 295 runs to Winsford from Lynton and Dulverton (tel. 01271 345444)

Round and About

The Devil and Caratacus

Find an ancient standing stone inscribed with the name Caratacus and thoughts turn to the brave British leader, usually spelt Caractacus, who resisted the Romans when they invaded in AD43. Although the stone may have been erected in the Bronze Age, its Latin inscription is dated to the fifth or sixth centuries AD. Translated as meaning 'Clansman of Caratacus', it could refer to Caradog Freichfras (Strong Arm), an uncle of King Arthur. Also known as Sir Craddock, he was the son of Gwrgant Mawr, King of Erging, who was also the father of Onbrawst, wife of Meurig, King of Gwent. Meurig was the father of King Arthur (and held the title Uther Pendragon). Caradog later ruled the Vannes area of Brittany, where he is celebrated as St Caradec.

Known as the Langestone, a forest boundary stone, in the Middle Ages, a longstanding belief that it marked the spot of buried treasure may have caused it to have been mysteriously moved in 1936. Re-erected on its original site, it now has a shelter. Temper admiration for the scenic beauty of the Punchbowl with care for whom you might meet near it! The Punchbowl resulted from the devil's great thirst after he had created Tarr Steps. Resting on

Winsford Hill, where there was no convenient stream, he decided to dig for water. Thus was created his Punchbowl, with the displaced soil being dumped in a mound to become Dunkery Hill.

The Caratacus Stone

The Walk

1. Take the road signposted for Tarr Steps, bearing left, away from the ford on your right. Climb to a signposted bridleway, a hedged track, which you turn left along. Follow this for one mile and enter woodland.

2. Go ahead through a gate, turn left over a stile and turn right to cross a footbridge and continue following the blue arrows of the waymarked bridleway. Climb through woodland, keeping above a stream on your right. Emerge through a gate onto open land.

3. Turn right, as signposted, to take the bridleway for Spire Cross and Tarr Steps. Walk with a hedge on your right, diverging from it to aim for a small wooden gate in the hedge ahead about 50 metres (45 yards) to the left of the corner. Bear half-left along a clear path through the bracken and heather moorland. Go ahead through a gate giving access to a road but go left before the road (walking with the road on your right) to come to the sheltered Caratacus Stone.

4. Turn right to reach a crossroads and go ahead along the B3223 in the direction of Exford and Withypool. It is possible to walk parallel to this road on the bracken-covered moorland. Reach a waymark post on your right and, ignoring a bridleway coming in sharply from your right, bear right along the bridleway for Withycombe.

5. Walk above the Punchbowl on your right, bearing right to descend to a gate. Continue with trees on your right. Bear right, as waymarked, to descend with the trees now on your left (with the Punchbowl now behind you on your right). Take a gate waymarked with blue paint on your left and continue descending along a track. Bear left with the access lane from Withycombe Farm.

6. After leaving the farmyard, do not take the access lane ahead up to a road. Instead, fork right along a public footpath, waymarked with yellow arrows and signposted for Winsford. Walk along the foot of a field with a hedge on your right. Go ahead through a gate in the corner and the next field to continue through a gateway in the hedge opposite. Walk with a hedge on your right in the third field, continue beside a line of trees, take a gate and go ahead with a hedge on your right. maintain this direction through a kissing-gate and with a fence on your right. Take an enclosed path ahead to reach a final field where a stile gives access to another enclosed path which leads to a gate on your left giving access to a road.

7. Go right along the road into Winsford.

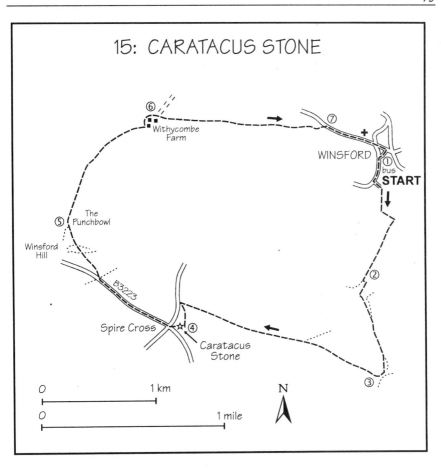

15: CARATACUS STONE

16. The Triscombe Stone

Route: Crowcombe Heathfield Station – Wills Neck – Triscombe Stone – Great Hill – Crowcombe Heathfield Station

Distance: 7 miles. Strenuous

Maps: O.S. Explorer 22 Quantock Hills and Bridgwater; O.S. Landranger 181 Minehead and Brendon Hills.

Start: Crowcombe Heathfield Station (ST136344).

Access: Trains run on the West Somerset Railway to Crowcombe Heathfield Station from Minehead and Bishops Lydeard (with bus connections to Taunton). Tel. 01643 704996 for details (including steam services).

Round and About

The Wild Hunt

Avoid the Triscombe Stone on stormy nights, when the Wild Hunt may be about. The devil himself is said to ride a black steed at the head of a pack of Wish-Hounds (distinguished by flame-red tongues). These are the spirits of the eternally damned. These tormented ones gain relief from their own sufferings by hunting down human souls to join them. The Wild Hunt is seen before the death of a witch, for instance. It features in a novel for children by Penelope Lively, *The Wild Hunt of Hagworthy*. The Wild Hunt is no idle threat. Consider this quotation from a member of Stogumber Women's Institute in 1960: 'The Yeff Hounds, or Ghost Pack, were heard pattering through Stogumber after midnight this year, but no one looked out to see them, even nowadays. They are known to turn through the village and down towards Roebuck, then up to Wills Neck.' (*Somerset Folklore* by R.L. Tongue, ed. K. Briggs, published by The Folklore Society in *County Folklore* Vol. VIII, 1965).

Crowcombe Heathfield station

The Walk

1. Go along the station access road to a junction with a road coming over a bridge on your left. Turn right to follow this road to the A358. Cross this road carefully and turn right to walk along its verge.

2. Turn left along a road heading for the Quantock Hills. Pass a turning to a garden centre on your right. Go right with a road signposted for Bagborough. Pass a pub on your right and turn right, as signposted for Bagborough. This road bends left.

3. Fork left along a track, go ahead through a gateway and turn left to climb with a steep path. Bear right at the top of the trees to join a path leading to the summit of Wills Neck.

4. Turn left to follow a path which descends, keeping a quarry on your left. Reach a car park and go left along a track.

5. The Triscombe Stone is on your left while a cattle grid marks the end of a road giving access to a car park on your right. Go ahead along the track for one mile. Pass a signposted public bridleway going through a gate on your right and heading for St David's Well. Shortly after this, take a small wooden gate next to a fieldgate on your left. Enter an open hillside and descend with a line of trees on your right. Continue through a farmyard.

6. Go straight downhill when you emerge on a road at a bend (i.e. bear right). Soon come to a fork, where you bear left. Reach a junction with another road and bear left along it. Reach the A358 and turn right along its verge for 135 metres (150 yards). Turn left to take a quiet lane towards the West Somerset Railway.

7. Go ahead over a level crossing and turn left, as signposted for Crowcombe Heathfield (1 mile). Ignore a turning on your right for Willett. Do turn left with the road to cross the bridge over the West Somerset Railway and go right to return to the station.

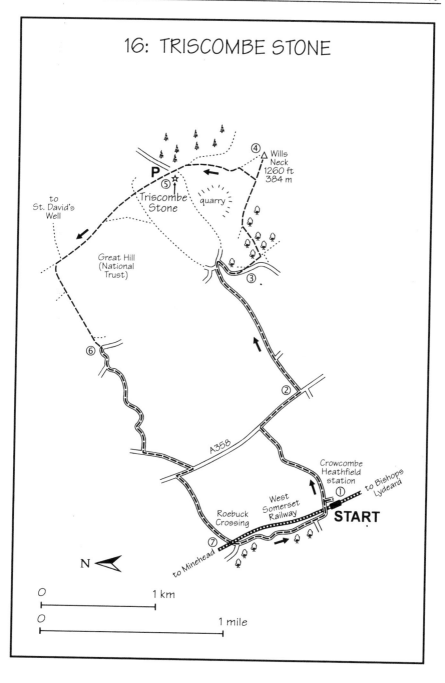

16: TRISCOMBE STONE

P

△ Wills
Neck
1260 ft
384 m

⑤ ☆
Triscombe
Stone

quarry

to
St. David's
Well

Great Hill
(National
Trust)

③

⑥

②

A358

Crowcombe
Heathfield
station
① to Bishops
Lydeard

West
Somerset
Railway

START

Roebuck
Crossing

⑦

to Minehead

N ◀

O   1 km

O   1 mile

17. Sedgemoor

Route: Westonzoyland – Chedzoy – King's Sedgemoor Drain – Battle of Sedgemoor Memorial – Westonzoyland

Distance: 6 miles. Easy.

Maps: O.S. Explorer 22 Quantock Hills; O.S. Landranger 182 Weston-super-Mare and Bridgwater.

Start: The Sedgemoor Inn, Westonzoyland (ST351348).

Access: Bus no. 16 runs to Westonzoyland from Bridgwater (tel. 01823 358299).

Round and About

A Case for Reincarnation

The Battle of Sedgemoor was fought on 6 July, 1685, on the wet-lands to the northern side of Westonzoyland. The desire for civil and religious liberty had led the Protestants of the West Country to rise up in support of James Scott, Duke of Monmouth, first but illegitimate son of Charles II, against James II, the autocratic Roman Catholic who had become king upon the death of his brother. Monmouth's army of about 7000 men was ill-equipped, leading to the description 'Pitchfork Rebellion'. When the royal army, led by the Earl of Feversham, came in pursuit of them, the Duke of Monmouth took a gamble by attempting to surprise the king's forces, which were camped at Westonzoyland, with a night attack from Bridgwater. Feversham had made precautions for such an event, the alarm was raised and the brave rebels were defeated. The locals counted 1384 corpses, most of whom were buried in a mass grave on the site now occupied by the war memorial. When trying to imagine the battlefield, note that the Bussex and Langmoor Rhines (pronounced 'reens' – drainage channels) have since been filled in, while King's Sedgemoor Drain, cut in the 1790s, absorbed the Black Ditch. The Duke of Monmouth fled from the battle but was captured and executed at Tower Hill, London, on 15 July. The notorious Judge Jeffreys came to the West Country and caused about 330 men to be executed and 849 transported to the West Indies. With dismembered corpses exhibited throughout Somerset, Devon and Dorset, it was said that the countryside in the West looked like a butcher's shop. Not surprisingly, there are ghost stories, especially of spectral soldiers and hoofbeats around the battlefield, either on 6 July or 17 July (allowing for the change in the calendar). Many ancient trees and crossroads are said to have grim, ghostly, reminders of hangings.

There is also a tale dating from 1680 when the Duke of Monmouth touched a local girl who was disfigured by scrofula, a tubercular disease known as the King's Evil because it was believed that it could only be cured by the touch of a king. The girl was cured, causing many to recognise the Duke of Monmouth as a true king. When a gipsy fortune-teller warned Monmouth to beware of the Rhine, however, he mistakenly felt secure in the belief that he was not going to campaign in Germany! He failed to realise that his Royalist opponents at Westonzoyland would be defended by the drainage channel known as Bussex Rhine.

A local woman, Elizabeth Winter from Chedzoy, was inspired to erect the memorial stone in 1928 after hearing an unearthly voice pointing out the 'unmourned and unremembered' in her fields.

The strangest of all the stories relating to the Battle of Sedgemoor is contained in the book *Second Time Round* by E.W. Ryall. This is an astonishingly detailed account of the retrieved memory of a previous life, that of John Fletcher, a yeoman farmer born in 1645, who was killed at the battle. He was guiding the vanguard of Monmouth's cavalry, which was some 90 metres (100 yards) from the Bussex Rhine when the whinny of a horse in the rebel line alerted a royalist cavalry patrol. John Fletcher died in the resulting skirmish. This is not necessarily at odds with the conventional story of how Monmouth's forces were betrayed by a pistol shot. The shot came from the royalist side after the horse's whinny. A Captain Hucker claimed to have fired his pistol as a warning to the king's forces, but he did so whilst pleading for mercy at his trial for treason. When, despite his claim, he came to stand at the gallows, he retracted it.

The Duke of Monmouth's local guide was named as Godfrey, Newton or Newman. He lost his way, however, so was dismissed and was not with the cavalry when it reached the Bussex Rhine. It is recorded that Lord Grey, the Duke of Monmouth's cavalry leader, had another guide with him as he approached the Bussex Rhine.

In a full and carefully-argued Introduction to E.W. Ryall's book, the eminent psychiatrist Dr Ian Stevenson concludes by believing it 'best interpreted as an instance of reincarnation. In other words, I think it most probable that he has memories of a real previous life and that he is indeed John Fletcher reborn, as he believes himself to be.'

According to E.W. Ryall/John Fletcher, there was an air of melancholy about the Duke on Sunday, 5 July, in Bridgwater. The blue banner with its motto 'Fear nothing but God' was exhibited to stiffen weakening resolves. That evening John walked back to Dunwear (ST317354), made love for the last time to his wife's sister Susannah, mounted his horse Pegasus and rode to the River Parrett. A molehill by the riverbank, combined with a lack of concentration brought on by John's deep thoughts, caused Pegasus to cast a shoe and become lame in the left fore. John spent that evening with Cecily, his wife. Cecily's lover, and John's friend, Jeremy Bragg called to ask John to guide the Duke's army across the moor to the further crossing of the Bussex Rhine, saying 'There is one who promises to lead us safely, for payment, but I and others trust him not, so I have come to ask if ye will aid us'. This was a reference to Godfrey.

As the sun set behind the Quantock Hills, a cloud crossed it and three gulls circled John's house three times before flying off across the moor with plaintive cries – three times three, the Nine tellers of a death of a man! After Jeremy had finished romping with Cecily, John went upstairs to make love to his wife for the last time. The two men set off just after 11 pm. When contact was made with the cavalry at the crossing over the Langmoor Rhine, it was discovered that Godfrey had deserted them. They met a royalist cavalry patrol on the northern side of the Bussex Rhine. A royalist trooper killed John, who was on foot, with his sword – 'a whistling sound, a great red flash and oblivion!'

Get in the mood at the Sedgemoor Inn before starting the walk!

The Walk

1. Face the Sedgemoor Inn and go left. Turn left immediately to follow the main road, turning right at the next corner. Leave the Westonzoyland road sign behind you and reach a cemetery on your left.

2. Turn right along a hedged track. About 45 metres (50 yards) before this makes a turn to the right, turn left through a gate and walk along the left-hand side of a field. Take a gap in the corner ahead and turn right to walk along the right-hand side of this field. Reach Chedzoy New Cut and cross it by a foot-bridge. Go ahead along the right-hand side of the next field.

3. Turn left along a track (Moor Drove). Follow this to the road at Fowler's Plot. Go right along this road to reach Chedzoy.

4. Just before Higher Road on your left, turn right along Frys Lane. When this ends, go ahead over a stile beside a gate and cross a field to reach another track (Moor Drove again). Turn right along this until you reach King's Sedgemoor Drain.

5. Turn right to walk with King's Sedgemoor Drain on your left. Cross a sluice-bridge for Chedzoy New Cut and continue to a stile beside a gate. Do not proceed! Turn right, away from the waterway, and follow a track which passes the war memorial to the Battle of Sedgemoor on your right.

6. Turn left to follow the track to Bussex Farm. Turn right along Monmouth Road. Pass Cheer Lane on your left. Soon after Bussex Stores on your left, turn left along an enclosed path to emerge between St Mary's Church on your left and the Sedge-moor Inn on your right.

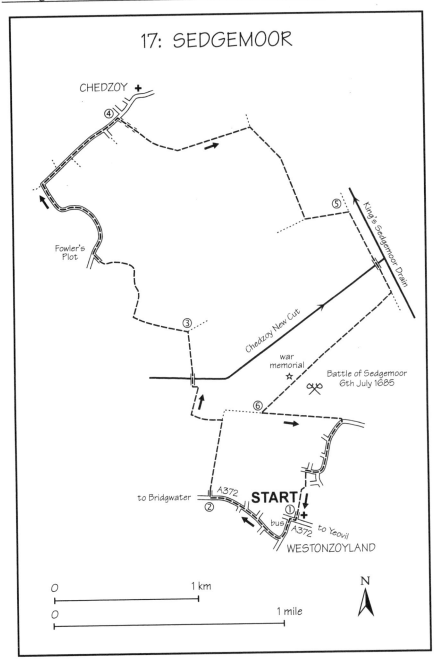

17: SEDGEMOOR

CHEDZOY ✝

④

⑤

King's Sedgemoor Drain

Fowler's
Plot

Chedzoy New Cut

③

war
memorial
☆

Battle of Sedgemoor
6th July 1685

⑥

to Bridgwater   A372   **START**

②

bus   A372   to Yeovil

WESTONZOYLAND

0 _____ 1 km

0 _____ 1 mile

N

18. Creech Hill

Route: Bruton – Creech Hill – Bruton

Distance: 4 miles. Strenuous.

Maps: O.S. Explorer 5 Mendip Hills East; O.S. Landranger 183 Yeovil and Frome.

Start: Bruton railway station (ST687348).

Access: Trains run to Bruton on the Bristol-Weymouth line (tel. 0345 484950). For details of local buses, tel. 01823 358299.

Round and About

A Bullbeggar

There is something special about Creech Hill. The Romans built a temple on it (ST669362), while it has been associated with all types of supernatural beasts and ghosts for centuries. Even in August, 1998, as I started my walk up it, I met a couple of locals and casually enquired if anything unusual was ever seen up this hill. Immediately, one man replied that his wife had seen a strange creature, like a black dog but much bigger, only three months before. I had not told him that a Black Dog has been seen here in the past (see Walk 27, Broadway for more about black dogs). A bullbeggar is a bogeyman that can suddenly shoot up to a great height. Fiendish shrieks of gleeful laughter are a characteristic of it. One chased a farmer home late one night as he made his way over Creech Hill. In pre-television days, of course, it was great fun to frighten your neighbours by standing on another's shoulders to impersonate a very tall ghost, but to do so with credibility demands the existence of authentic originals. As the man I spoke to emphasised to me with some wonderment, his wife was sure she hadn't seen an ordinary black dog ....

The Walk

1. Go down the station access road, turn right along Station Road and pass St Mary's Church on your left. Go right to cross Church Bridge over the River Brue, bear left up Patwell Street and turn left along Bruton High Street.

2. Turn right along Mill Dam (an alleyway). Go right at a junction at a ford to climb with a lane but leave this before it bends right. Turn left along a hedged path. Cross a footbridge to the right of a ford, go right and almost immediately turn left up a

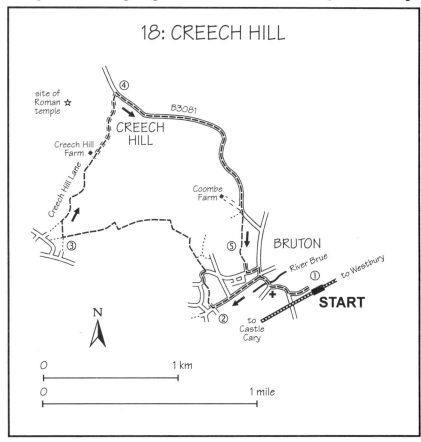

18: CREECH HILL

site of Roman ☆ temple

B3081

CREECH HILL

Creech Hill Farm ◆

Creech Hill Lane

Coombe Farm ◆

BRUTON

River Brue   to Westbury

START

to Westbury

N

to Castle Cary

O   1 km

O   1 mile

hedged path. Follow this for nearly one mile, ignoring a way-marked stile on your left.

3. Turn right through double gates to take a broad, fenced, track which passes farm buildings on your left before a gate ahead gives access to Creech Hill Lane. Turn right up this hedged track which becomes metalled after passing Creech Hill Farm on your left.

4. Turn right to follow the B3081 road downhill. Pass the drive to Coombe Farm on your right and ignore a signposted public footpath immediately after it. Go ahead 18 metres (20 yards), turn right across a stile and bear half-left to follow the sign-posted public footpath to Bruton. Climb to cross a stile in a fence ahead and descend beside woodland on your right.

5. Bear right to take a walled passage and go downhill with a wall on your left in the next field. Go ahead over a stile and down an enclosed path. Turn left along a road (Higher Backway), then turn right down Coombe Street. Pass Quaperlake Street on your left. Turn left down Patwell Street to retrace your steps over Church Bridge to Bruton railway station.

19. Fyne Court

Route: Kingston St Mary – Fyne Court – Cothelston Hill – Bishops Lydeard

Distance: 9 miles (linear route between bus stops). Strenuous.

Maps: O.S. Explorer 22 Quantock Hills and Bridgwater; O.S. Landrangers (3 maps) 181 Minehead and Brendon Hills, 182 Weston-super-Mare and Bridgwater and 193 Taunton and Lyme Regis.

Start: Post Office, Kingston St Mary, bus stop for no. 23 (ST221296).

Finish: Newsagent's shop, Bishops Lydeard, bus stop for no. 28A (ST169299).

Access: Bus no. 23 from Taunton to start in Kingston St Mary. Bus no. 28A from finish in Bishops Lydeard back to Taunton, or bus no. 28 (Taunton-Minehead), tel. 01823 358299 for bus times. Trains run from Bishops Lydeard to Minehead on the West Somerset Railway, tel. 01643 704996.

Round and About

The Home of Frankenstein

Fyne Court was the home of the pioneer electrician Andrew Crosse (1784-1855). The house was destroyed by fire in 1894 but the stables and music room survived and now house the headquarters of the Somerset Wildlife Trust and a visitor centre for the Quantocks. Admission is daily and free. Known as the Wizard of Broomfield, Andrew Crosse was the inspiration for Mary Shelley's *Frankenstein or the Modern Prometheus*, published in 1818.

The Walk

1. With your back to the post office, cross the road and go straight ahead up Lodes Lane. Climb to a T-junction where you initially turn right along the road for Netherton but, after just nine metres (10 yards), turn left along a hedged path which is waymarked by a red arrow. Ignore tracks going through gates into woodland on your right. Continue along the hedged path to emerge on a road at a bend in it. Go left along the road to pass Broomfield church on your right. Turn right along the signposted lane to Fyne Court.

2. Go back down the lane and turn right to resume your previous direction along the road. Turn right at a T-junction and bear left when this road forks. Immediately, just before a telephone box, turn left to take a signposted public right of way with a red arrow waymark again. Reach a fork in this old green lane and bear right along the higher path. Ford a stream and emerge beside a road at Raswell Farm.

3. Go right along the road for half a mile. Turn left along a sign-posted public footpath (yellow arrow) which goes through a gate and follows a forest path above a stream on your left. Ig-nore tracks forking right uphill into the forest.

4. Turn left to cross the stream and reach a ruin on your left. When level with this ruin, turn right along a woodland path. As you approach the edge of the wood, paths converge on yours from the right. Reach a path running alongside the pe-rimeter hedge of the wood at a waymarked junction. Turn right to follow it, keeping just inside the wood. Emerging from the wood, do not fork left along a waymarked bridleway. Bear right to take a gate onto the open access land of Cathelstone Hill. Go ahead along a permissive bridleway, ignoring tracks going right. Reach a waymarked public footpath and fork right to climb with it to the summit. Maintain this direction down the other side to reach a stile to the left of a gate in the perime-ter fence of the woodland which fringes this hill. Go ahead over it, take a woodland path and emerge onto a road.

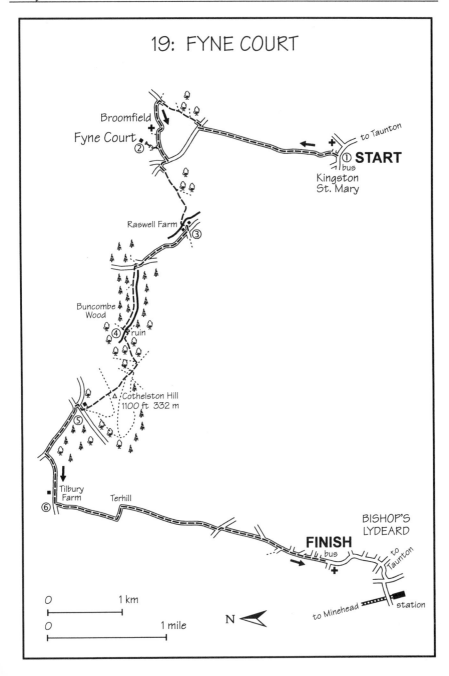

19: FYNE COURT

Broomfield

Fyne Court

② to Taunton

① **START**
bus
Kingston
St. Mary

Raswell Farm ③

Buncombe
Wood ④ ruin

△ Cothelston Hill
1100 ft 332 m

⑤

Tilbury
Farm ⑥ Terhill

BISHOP'S
LYDEARD

FINISH
bus
to Taunton

0   1 km

0   1 mile

N

to Minehead   station

5. Go right to a road junction and turn left, as signposted for Bagborough. Ignore a turning for Bishpool on your right. Go ahead for half a mile, then turn left as signposted for West Bagborough. Pass Tilbury Farm on your right.

6. Turn left down a steep lane. Pass Pilgrims Cottage on your right. Follow the lane through Terhill, going under an arch as you continue to descend southwards. Reach a junction with a lower road. Go left for 27 metres (30 yards), then turn right to descend to a junction with a road coming sharply from your left. Go right, as signposted for Bishops Lydeard. The village is soon entered and the no. 28A bus will stop by request from the papershop near the junction with West Street on your right.

20. Burrow Mump

Route: Westonzoyland – Middlezoy – Burrow Mump – Hoopers Elm Farm – Westonzoyland

Distance: 8½ miles. Easy (except for the climb up Burrow Mump).

Maps: O.S. Explorer 22 Quantock Hills; O.S. Landranger 182 Weston-super-Mare and Bridgwater.

Start: The Sedgemoor Inn, Westonzoyland (ST351348).

Access: Bus no. 16 runs to Westonzoyland from Bridgwater (tel. 01823 358299).

Round and About

A Sop to Cerberus?

Burrow, or Burrowbridge, Mump was used as a look-out post by King Alfred when nearby Athelney (ST346293) became his last refuge against the Danes in 878. Here, on an island in the marshes, is where Alfred burnt the famous cakes. But there's more to this story of cakes than meets the eye!

The Mump is thought by some to be a focal point for leys or lines of 'dragon energy'. St Michael – legendary slayer of dragons – is said to have tamed these bearing the 'sword of the Will', He is a guide to the pathway between life and death and The Mump is appropriately crowned by the ruins of a church dedicated to St Michael. The site of this church's altar is, according to *The Sun and the Serpent* by Hamish Miller and Paul Broadhurst, where Michael and Mary currents cross. The Great Dragon Line, traced in their book from Cornwall to Norfolk, goes at an angle of 63 degrees (sunrise line in early May and early August, corresponding to Beltane and Lugnasadh) through the Mump on its way to Glastonbury Tor. Like the Tor, the Mump appears to have been artificially shaped and terraced, while their major axes align with each

Burrow Mump

other. The 11 miles from Burrow Mump to Glastonbury Tor form
one side of a rhombus. The Mump is its easterly point, the Tor its
northern, Cadbury Castle its westerly point and Hamdon Hill its
southern. The 11 miles from Hamdon Hill to Burrow Mump are at
an angle of 320 degrees, being the line of the moonset in the
northerly major standstill.

Somerset legends refer to a 'girt dog' haunting the marshes
with its snout forming the Mump and its tail at Wagg, near Langport (Walk 23). This giant landscape figure lies outside the wheel
of the Glastonbury Zodiac. Like a guardian dog, it faces the seaward approach from the Bristol Channel. Its underside is deline-
ated by the River Parrett (= Pharat from Euphrates –
Sumerian/Phoenician). Perhaps Hercules (a Phoenician before
the Greeks adopted him) strangled Cerberus here, at the mouth of
Hades. Can we say, perhaps a little tongue-in-cheek, that Alfred
burnt the cakes as he was preparing a 'sop to Cerberus'? Is this

where he was initiated into the Mysteries, with the burning of barley cakes being an ancient solar custom?

Alfred was a Celt, rather than a Saxon. He was descended from Cerdic (a form of Caradoc or Caractacus) of the Gewissae (the Wise Ones, perhaps Gnostics) and Wessex is named after the Gewissae, not the West Saxons. Alfred was advised by druids, notably the Welsh monk Asser. Significantly, after he defeated his Danish opponent Guthrum, Alfred made peace with him. Dividing the country between himself and Guthrum, he insisted on Guthrum travelling from Chippenham to Aller (on the girt dog's back, just to the east of Burrow Mump) to be baptised as a Christian and to be received by Alfred as his adoptive son. Was Guthrum initiated here too? It's interesting to surmise, but we shall never know!

The Walk

1. Face the Sedgemoor Inn and go right to pass St Mary's Church on your left. Follow the main road to the eastern edge of Westonzoyland. When you reach Liney Road on your left, turn right along a hedged track.

2. Bear right at a fork and follow Langmead Drove, a track through the wetlands, as it bends left, then right, then left again. Ignore a stile beside a gate straight ahead at the next corner. Turn right with what becomes a roughly-metalled lane. Follow this as it turns left towards Middlezoy.

3. Reach a major junction and turn sharply right along a hedged (muddy) track. Emerge at a road T-junction. Ignore Holloway Road which goes straight ahead. Turn right and at the next road junction in Thorngrove turn left. Follow this road as it turns left at a corner occupied by Wayside Cottage on your left, ignoring tracks going straight ahead and right.

4. As the road bends right, leave it to go straight ahead along a

signposted RUPP (road used as a public path). This is Broad
Drove, a grassy track. Turn right at a junction with another
grassy track, Burrow Drove. Notice Burrow Mump ahead on
your left. Join a lane and go left to walk downstream with the
River Parrett on your right. Reach the main road which
crosses the river by a bridge on your right. King Alfred Inn is
ahead, across the road. Turn left and reach the village school
on your left. Look for steps on your right (marked by a plaque
to Edward Storey). These lead to a gate and a climb up to the
ruined church dedicated to St Michael that crowns this dis-
tinctive hill.

5. Retrace your steps down Burrow Mump and to the King Alfred Inn. Do not cross the bridge. Turn right to follow the lane,
   this time walking upstream with the River Parrett on your left.
   Pass Burrow Drove on your right. Continue past the lane to
   Thorngrove on your right.

6. Turn left with the road signposted for Westonzoyland and
   pass Hoopers Elm Farm on your right. Ignore a left turning to
   Andersea as you continue to Westonzoyland and the Sedgemoor Inn.

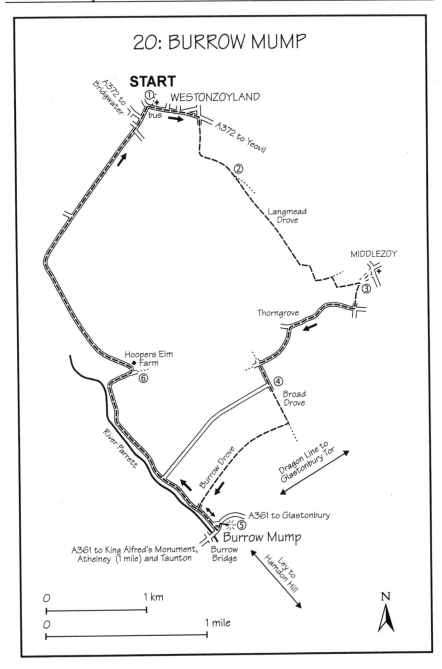

20: BURROW MUMP

21. Dundon Hill

Route: Compton Dundon – Hayes Lane – Dundon – Compton Dundon

Distance: 4 miles. Moderate.

Maps: O.S. Explorer 4 Mendip Hills West; O.S. Landranger 182 Weston-super-Mare and Bridgwater.

Start: Bus stop near the staggered crossroads in Compton Dundon (ST438639).

Access: Bus no. 376 (Bristol-Yeovil) runs through Compton Dundon (tel. 01823 358299).

Round and About

The Young Jesus

The aerial photograph in Mary Caine's *The Glastonbury Zodiac* highlights the possible significance of the paths around these parts. Here, in the sign of Cancer, we may see the young Jesus, seemingly cradled in a crescent-shaped ship. The moon rules this water-sign, while here is a reminder of how Joseph of Arimathea brought the young Jesus to Glastonbury. This walk begins by following the underside of Jesus' raised and bent right arm. Going down Jesus' face, it then follows Hayes Lane, marking the outside of Jesus' folded left arm. Forking right along the track towards Lollover Hill brings you to this giant landscape figure's wrist, where you turn to walk east along the old green lane to Dundon. Intriguingly, you walk along the raised lower half of Jesus' right arm back to the bus stop in Compton Dundon.

The Walk

1. Take Ham Lane, going west from the staggered crossroads where the B3151 runs through Compton Dundon. After 225

metres (250 yards), reach a house called Hood View on your
left. Turn left immediately after it to take a waymarked public
footpath which runs between houses to emerge through a gate
into a field. Bear half-left to continue beside the hedge on your
left and cross a stile in the far left-hand corner of this field.

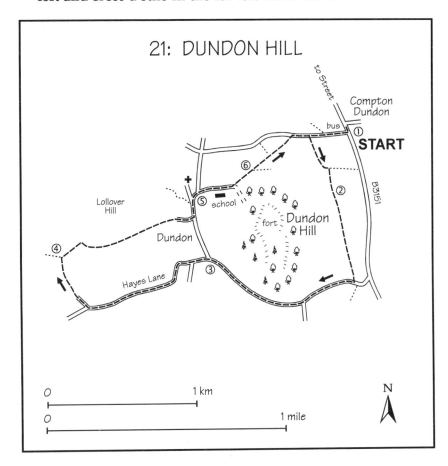

2. Go ahead, ignoring a stile beside a gate in the corner on your
left. Continue with the hedge on your left through this and
three more fields. Reach a lane and go right. Ignore an access
lane to a farm on your left. Bear right with the lane into the village of Dundon.

3. Fork left along Hayes Lane, ignore a turning on your left and go ahead up the No Through Road. When this bears left, fork right up a hedged track.

4. Ignore a stile beside a gate on your left. Turn right with the old green lane to follow it back to the road in Dundon, where you turn left.

5. Bear right with the road when the drive to the church goes straight ahead. Fork right along a No Through Road to pass the school on your right. Continue along a grassy, hedged, track. Pass a waymarked footpath on your right then, when the track turns right towards the woodland, go ahead through a kissing-gate to walk beside a hedge on your left.

6. Bear left through a kissing-gate and continue to another kissing-gate in the hedge ahead about 45 metres (50 yards) to the left of the corner on your right. Go ahead along an enclosed path and through a series of kissing-gates to emerge on a field where you maintain your direction to reach a road (Ham Lane). Go right to return to the crossroads and bus stop.

22. Babcary

Route: Barton St David – Babcary – Kingsdon

Distance: 8 miles (linear route, between bus stops). Easy.

Maps: O.S. Explorers 4 Mendip Hills West and 129 Yeovil and Sherborne; O.S. Landranger 182 Yeovil and Frome.

Start: The crossroads, Barton St David (ST542319).

Finish: Kingsdon post office (ST516261).

Access: Bus no. 167 runs to Barton St David from Wells. Buses nos 54 (Taunton-Yeovil) and 376 (Bristol-Wells-Yeovil) serve Kingsdon. Tel. 01823 358299 for details.

Round and About

Wimble Toot

Several signs of the Glastonbury Zodiac are traversed on this excellent linear walk. We start at Barton St David in the sign of Libra on the Zodiac. A giant landscape figure of a dove dives down, bringing light, spirit and divine mercy to some – or an interesting aspect of the countryside to others. To believers, this is the Dove of the Annunciation, Noah's Dove and the Awen of the Druids. An intermediary between God and Man, the dove is thought of as a 'diva', an angel-messenger from heaven to earth. Both 'dove' and 'David' may come from 'Duw Dofyddl, Welsh for God's Messenger. Inside Barton St David's Church is a picture of a harp – a Jewish one, for King David. St Columba was also a dove, metaphorically speaking, conveying the word from heaven to earth. Columbus forged a connecting column between Europe and America, to sustain colonies. Two American presidents, the Adams father and son, have a memorial in the church near their old family farmhouse.

The Triple Goddess

Walking south along Babcary Lane, we continue along the famed mystical zodiac to step onto Virgo's Triple Goddess. Located just below Barton St David's Libran Dove, we perceive the logos announcing her coming Virgin-birth. She is also old Mother Cary consorting with Davey Jones. Her swelling womb is marked by Babcary, where a local legend states that a royal child was hidden long ago. This was Henry II during the wars of Stephen and Matilda. Virgo's nipple is the tumulus known as Wimble Toot Wimble means an auger (a carpenter's bore). Is this a memory of augury or divination? Toot is possibly derived from the Welsh 'twt' for look-out mound, though 'toot' is also similar to the present-day 'teat'

Keinton Mandeville is the town of Virgo's hand. It is on the wheatsheaf or cornucopia of Ceres or Ceridwen, who was represented in the mystical Arthurian times by St Keyne.

Further along this walk, you step on to brush the foot of our landscape Leo as you take the lane to Kingsdon. Leo, the King of the Jungle, spreads itself over the old capital of Somerton. Here is the Arthurian Lancelot and Lughnasadh's Llew. His Lance of Light and hot heart seduce the nearby Earth Mother.

The Walk

1. Go along Church Street into the village of Barton St David. Pass Gregory's Orchard on your right as the road turns left to the church. Go left when facing the church. Go right at the main road (High Lane). Ignore Blind Lane bearing left. Go right up Peacock's Hill. Reach the gates of Northfield House on your right and turn left to take a track which has a hedge on your right. When you come to a gate giving access to a farmyard take the stile to its right to follow a narrow path beside the hedge. Maintain this direction in a field, keeping the hedge on your right. Notice Glastonbury Tor away to your left. Cross a stile in the corner and go ahead through the next field to reach a road.

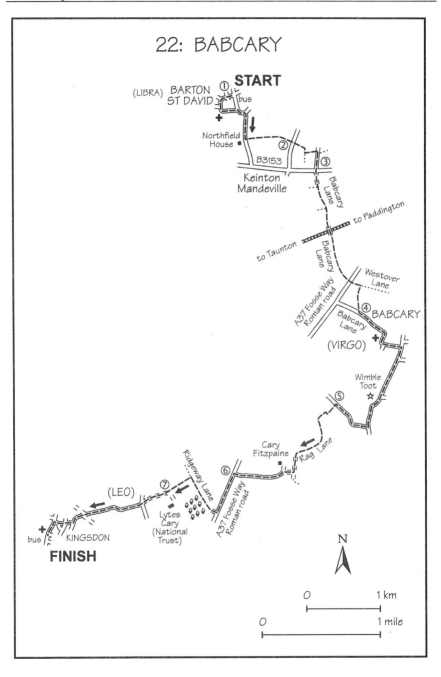

22: BABCARY

(LIBRA) BARTON ST DAVID ① START
bus

Northfield House ■
②

B3153
Keinton Mandeville
③
Babcary Lane

to Paddington

to Taunton
Babcary Lane

A37 Fosse Way Roman road

Westover Lane

④ BABCARY
Babcary Lane
(VIRGO)

Wimble Toot ☆

⑤

Cary Fitzpaine
Rag Lane

Ridgeway Lane
⑥

(LEO) ⑦

Lytes Cary (National Trust)

A37 Fosse Way Roman road

bus KINGSDON
FINISH

N

0 ___ 1 km

0 ___ 1 mile

2. Cross the road to take the old green lane ahead. This bends right to a house and continues as a narrow, hedged, path which passes the house on your left. Turn left when you reach a stone stile in the hedge on your left. Cross this stile and go ahead along the left-hand edges of two fields, then along an enclosed path to a road. Turn right along this.

3. Go straight ahead across the B3153 road to follow Babcary Lane. This is a No Through Road which soon deteriorates into an old green lane. cross the railway by a bridge and continue to the Fosse Way (A37). Cross this carefully and go ahead along another old green lane (Westover Lane). Turn right at a junction with a similar lane and reach a road.

4. Go left along this road (Babcary Lane again). Follow it through the village of Babcary, passing the Church of the Holy Cross on your right and ignoring a turning on your right. Reach a junction where you face the Red Lion Inn and turn right. Pass a turning on your left, then a waterworks on your right. Pass a turning for Little Steart House on your left and look out now for a gateway on your right. This gives you a view of Wimble Toot, a mound clothed by trees, in the field on your right. Continue along the road to a junction where you turn right, as signposted for Charlton Mackrell. After nearly half a mile, go downhill to where the hedge on your right doubles in height and there are gates on both left and right.

5. Take the gate on your left and walk along the left-hand edge of a field, away from the road. Continue around a jutting corner on your left, reach a gap in the hedge on your left and turn left through it to walk with a hedge on your right in this adjacent field. Go ahead along what becomes a green lane between hedges (Rag Lane). Follow this to a farm access lane (serving Cary Fitzpaine) and take this to the A37 (Fosse Way).

6. Cross the A37 carefully and turn left along its verge for half a mile. Turn right along an old green lane (Ridgeway Lane).

Look out for a signposted gap in the hedge on your left. Turn left to follow the signposted public bridleway through the field towards Lytes Cary (National Trust). Reach a corner formed by two hedges ahead and continue with a hedge on your left. Take a gap in the corner ahead.

7. Turn left through a gap to reach the drive for the National Trust's Lytes Cary. If you wish to visit this old manor house, go left, otherwise go right to follow the drive to the road. Turn left and almost immediately turn right to go down the road signposted for Kingsdon. Ignore a lane forking right ahead and another coming sharply from your left. Fork right at the edge of the village to follow the main road, passing turnings to right, left, then left again. Reach a T-junction where you go left to pass below the church on your right and reach the post office and bus stop.

23. Low Ham

Route: Langport — Huish Episcopi — Paradise — Low Ham — Wagg — Huish Episcopi — Langport

Distance: 6 miles. Easy.

Maps: O.S. Explorer 129 Yeovil and Sherborne; O.S. Landranger 193 Taunton and Lyme Regis.

Start: Town Hall, Langport (ST419268).

Access: Buses to Langport include no. 54 (Taunton-Langport-Somerton-Yeovil), tel. 01823 272033.

Round and About

A Dog and a New Model Army

What is the name of the place at the tip of the Girt Dog of Langport's tail? Why, Wagg, of course! Read Mary Caine's book *The Glastonbury Zodiac* to find out more, including where paths on this route outline it. Here, too, you go along Paradise Lane. Is this the Paradise known to the Initiates (those who were candidates for initiation into the mysteries of the region) and which the dog is said to guard? Mythologically, the dog guards Death's Door, leading both to heaven and hell.

About 300 Royalists were untimely despatched to one or other destination on 10 July, 1645. They died at the Battle of Langport when they came up against the New Model Army under the command of the redoubtable Sir Thomas Fairfax. A man of destiny, Thomas, Lord Fairfax, organized the New Model Army, with Cromwell serving under him. A moderate man, known for his commonsense and riding his white horse, Fairfax refused the opportunity to take the crown. He also declined to take part in the trial of the king and helped restore Charles II to the throne. He was essentially a soldier, rather than a politician. A humble, modest man with a stammer, he was the greatest general in

Europe. Adored by his soldiers, he had a strange mixture of dash and diffidence. Langport was a risky battle carried out with determination. Tall, wearing black armour, Fairfax had long dark brown hair, big eyes, a neat moustache, a pointed beard and a gentle face.

A Spear that killed a Dragon

Flying immediately above the Girt Dog's back, as it were, was a dragon. It would empty milkmaids' pails, suck cows dry and partake, even, of human flesh. A nearby knight, the gallant John Aller, plastered himself with pitch and wore a thick mask, took a long spear and attacked the dragon while it slept. The village of Aller is said to have been named after our hero, but you must go to the strangely isolated Low Ham Church to see his nine-feet long spear. Yes, you can actually handle a spear that killed a dragon! Low Ham was also famous for its fiddler. He once played for the devil (who was in disguise), learned of the devil's plans for the evil Lord Stawell and was able to warn the lord, who mended his ways 'in the nick of time'.

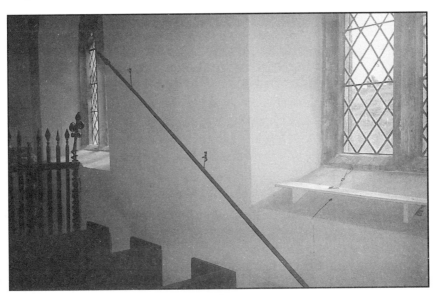

The spear that slew a dragon?

The Walk

1. With your back to the Town Hall, go left along Cheapside and fork right up The Hill. Pass All Saints' Church, Langport, on your right. Continue under an arch and along the pavement of the road to Huish Episcopi, where you pass St Mary's Church on your left. Pass the A372 going towards Bridgwater on your left. Go straight ahead, as signposted for Yeovil. Pass the Rose and Crown pub on your left.

2. Immediately after the Rose and Crown, turn left up Pounsell Lane. When this bears right, go straight ahead through a gate and along a footpath which keeps to the left-hand edge of the first field. Continue over a stile beside a gate in the corner and follow the path to the railway line. Cross this with great care and go ahead along the hedged path to reach a road.

3. Go left for 27 metres (30 yards) and turn right down steps to follow the tree-lined path ahead. Continue through a gate, then along a drive to meet a road. Turn left uphill.

4. Turn right along Paradise Lane. Ignore a turning on your left. Go ahead with Paradise Lane, passing the entrance to a firing range on your left. Turn right at the next road junction. Go left at another road junction to walk downhill to Low Ham. Turn right along a path to the isolated church on your right. You may have to ask at a nearby farmhouse for the key. The spear should be hanging inside the church's southern wall.

5. With your back to the church door, go left to take the path uphill, continue through a gate and reach a road. Turn right and bear left at a road junction, as signposted for Langport. Pass a turning for Wearne on your right. At the next road junction turn left, as signposted for Somerton, for 45 metres (50 yards).

6. Turn right along a track (Union Drove). Follow this over a

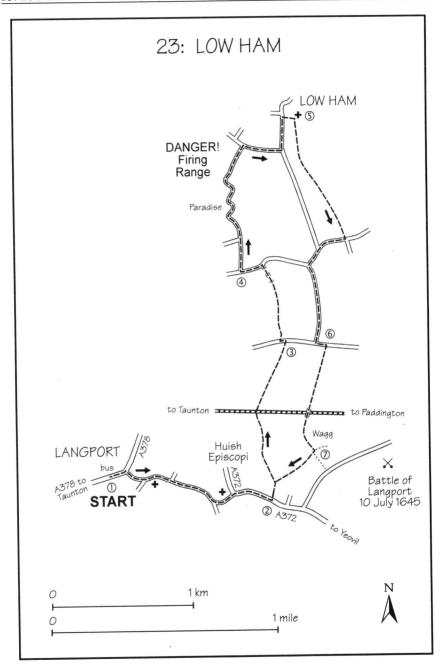

23: LOW HAM

bridge across the railway. Go ahead to a fork where you bear left downhill to Wagg.

7. Turn right over a stile and follow a path running between the backs of houses on your left and a fence on your right (ignore a stile in this). Go ahead over a stile to walk with a line of willows on your left, then past the backs of houses on your left. Return to the gate in the corner taken on your outward route. Go left through this and retrace your steps past the Rose and Crown and through Huish Episcopi to Langport.

24. Muchelney Abbey

Route: Langport – River Parrett Trail – Muchelney Abbey – Langport

Distance: 4 miles. Easy.

Maps: O.S. Explorer 129 Yeovil and Sherborne; O.S. Landranger 193 Taunton and Lyme Regis.

Start: Town Hall, Langport (ST419268).

Access: Buses to Langport include no. 54 (Taunton-Langport-Somerton-Yeovil), tel. 01823 272033.

Round and About

Down the Dog's Leg

The left-hand leg of the Girt Dog of Langport, the Glastonbury Zodiac's celebrated Cerberus, almost reaches down to the site of Muchelney Abbey. Drayton's *Polyolbion* (1612) contains these interesting lines with a reference to the River Parrett (= Pharat from Euphrates – Sumerian/Phoenician):

> *'For from the Druides' Time*
> *there was a prophecie*
> *That there should come a time*
> *(which now was near at hand*
> *By all fore-running signes)*
> *that on the eastern strand*
> *If Parrett stoode not firm upon*
> *the English side*
> *They all should be supprest.'*

Something here must be worth preserving, as Arviragus, Arthur and Alfred apparently knew. Langport was once a prosperous inland port (and noted for its freshwater mussels). It was put forward as a possible site for the Battle of Llongborth (perhaps in 508), when Geraint was slain fighting the Saxons, but it is more likely that a later Geraint died fighting the Saxons here in the early eighth century. Langport became a key point in Alfred's line of defence against the Danes. A Benedictine abbey was started here in 939 on the site of an early eighth century foundation. This is now in the care of English Heritage and can be visited (admission fee). Muchelney Abbey was the second oldest, after Glastonbury, of the 23 monastic foundations in Somerset at the Dissolution.

The Parrett Trail, Langport

The Walk

1. With your back to Langport Town Hall, go ahead across the road, pass a shopping arcade on your right and enter a car park, where you bear left to leave by a path which turns right to reach the River Parrett at a path signpost. Go left to walk upstream with the river on your right, passing a footbridge across a backwater on your left. Reach Huish Bridge (a footbridge) and turn right to cross it.

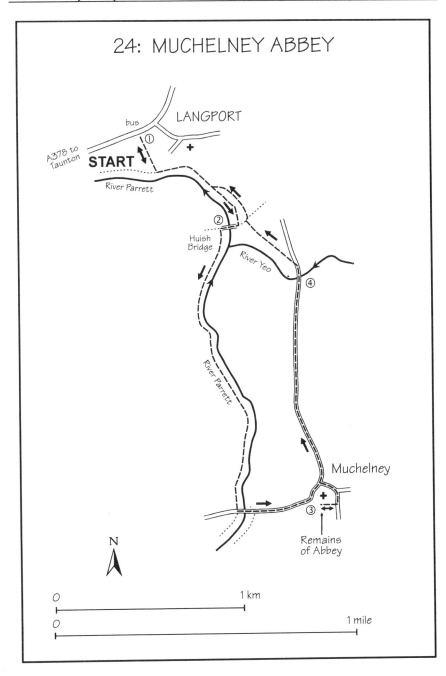

24: MUCHELNEY ABBEY

2. Turn left to walk along the waymarked River Parrett Trail, going upstream with the river on your left. Reach a road and turn left along it to cross the river by a bridge and reach Muchelney. Pass the parish church of St Peter and St Paul on your right. Pass for the moment the road to Langport on your left, then the Priest's House (National Trust). Follow the road around to the right and turn right, as signposted, to visit the remains of Muchelney Abbey (English Heritage).

3. Either retrace your steps along the River Parrett Trail into Langport or return to the road junction in Muchelney, with the church now on your left. If you wish to take a different route back, go right along the road to Langport. NB The public footpath marked on the O.S. maps along the eastern side of the River Parrett, then the southern side of the River Yeo, was walked by the author but found to be made too unpleasant by nettles.

4. Cross the bridge over the River Yeo. Look out for a waymarked public footpath bearing left over a stile. Follow this to a lane leading to Huish Bridge on your left. Go straight ahead across this lane to take a stile and walk with a backwater on your left until a footbridge across it. Turn left over this footbridge, then go right to retrace your steps into Langport.

25. Chilton Cantelo

Route: Ilchester – Yeovilton – Chilton Cantelo – Ashington – Limington – Ilchester

Distance: 9 miles. Easy.

Maps: O.S. Explorer 129 Yeovil and Sherborne; O.S. Landranger 183 Yeovil and Frome.

Start: Ilchester Town Hall (ST522227).

Access: Buses to Ilchester include no. 54 (Taunton-Yeovil) and no. 376 (Bristol-Yeovil), tel. 01823 358299.

Round and About

A Screaming Skull

Opposite St James's Church, Chilton Cantelo, is Higher Farm. This private residence houses a 'screaming skull'. Polite enquirers may be allowed an appointment to view it upon advance application (in writing, enclosing an s.a.e.) to Mr and Mrs Kerton – please do not disturb them without a prior written appointment. The skull is said to be that of Theophilus Broome, who died in 1670, aged 69. His tomb is inside the church but, conforming with local tradition (and with the ancient Celtic cult of the head?), he asked that his head be preserved at the farmhouse near the church. An attempt to bury the skull reputedly led to the spade breaking, while the skull has been alleged to scream when other attempts have been made to move it from old Theophilus's chosen resting-place.

Roman Reminders

Ilchester was once a Roman fort (chester) on the River Yeo (or Ivel). The Romans called it Lendinis, at the junction of the Fosse Way (Lincoln – Axmouth, Devon) and a road going from Dorchester to the Bristol Channel. Mendip lead was carried across the ford here. Ivel (or Yeo) could refer to Eve or Guinevere (White Eve). The patriarchal Roman Church may see her as Evil because it fears her charms. She is loved by many good Yeomen, however.

The Walk

1. With your back to Ilchester Town Hall, bear right to cross the top of Church Street carefully and turn sharply right along Back Lane. When this turns right, go left to walk between walls, up and down steps, then through a kissing-gate on your right. Follow the signposted Leland Trail (and the Monarch's Way), passing the River Yeo (Ivel) on your left and walking with a hedge on your left, ignoring a gate in it. Go ahead over a waymarked stile in the corner, follow a hedge on your left, cross stiles and a footbridge to the next field, where you head for the far left corner ahead. Cross a track, cut through a corner of a field and climb to join a hedge on your right. Go ahead over a stile and to the far left-hand corner of the following field, where you cross a stile to the right of a gate, then bear left to cross a stream by a bridge.

2. Turn right to walk with the stream on your right. Go ahead across a footbridge over a sluice feeding a drainage channel. Take a small wooden gate in the corner ahead, ignoring a footbridge on your right. Bear slightly left to cross a meadow diagonally to join a road and turn left with it across a bridge over the River Yeo (Ivel). Follow the road towards Yeoviltown.

3. Just before the first house, turn right to follow the waymarked Leland Trail. Ignore a footbridge across the river on your right. Continue past the Royal Naval Air Station on your left. Turn right over a footbridge across a tributary (the River Cam) and go left to walk upstream with this river and the helicopter base on your left. When the Cam bends right, away from the military airfield, follow it, ignore a footbridge across it but do turn

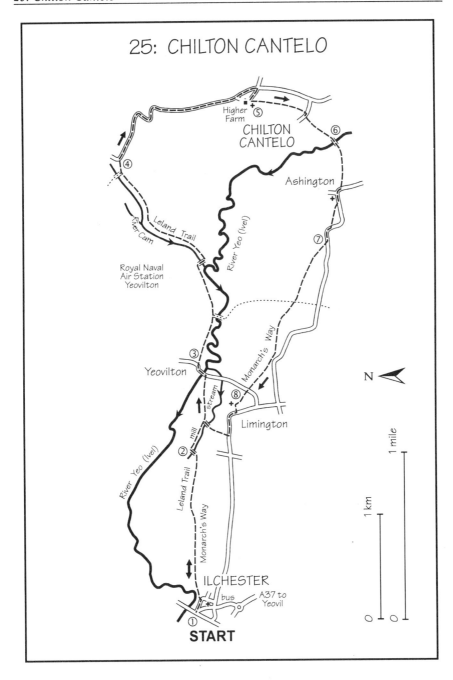

25: CHILTON CANTELO

left to follow the way-
marked Leland Trail
through a gate and along
the left side of a field.
Reach a bridge on your
left and bear right to
come to a road.

4. Go right along the road.
Reach Chilton Cantelo
and turn right at the
crossroads to follow the
access road to the church
(and Higher Farm).

5. Just before the church,
turn left along a narrow
path past the churchyard
on your right, then with a
high wall on your right.
Continue across a track

On the Leland Trail, east of Ilchester

and go ahead along a
hedged path. Emerge at a road and go right for 36 metres (40
yards), then turn left over a stile to take a narrow, hedged,
path. Enter a field and bear slightly left to reach a footbridge
across the River Yeo (Ivel).

6. Cross the river, continue along the right-hand edge of a field
and bear right at a road to follow it through Ashington. Pass
the church and Manor Cottage on your right, then bear right
over a stile to follow the waymarked Monarch's Way as it cuts
across the corner of a field. Take a stile on your left to rejoin
the road and go right along it for 180 metres (200 yards).

7. Fieldpaths are followed by the Monarch's Way (a 609-mile
route from Worcester to Shoreham in the footsteps of King

Charles II) to Limington. They are paralleled by a road. When the author walked this route in July, 1998, it has to be pointed out that the footpaths became an endurance test because of impenetrable oil-seed rape. The Monarch's Way does follow legal rights of way and it should be free of obstructions, even by crops. The more feet along it the better, so it is described here. However, the fainthearted have been warned! So, if you are not taking the road all the way into Limington, turn right through the second gate on your right and bear half-left through a field. Cross a stile in the next field, maintain your direction to take doublegates out of this and walk with a hedge on your left in the third field. Continue through a gap to bear slightly right through a fourth field, cross a footbridge over a ditch and reach an old green lane (Hook Drove). Go straight across this to go over a waymarked stile in the next corner and maintain this direction through the following field. Continue through a gap near its left-hand corner ahead (where a gate gives access to the road). Bear half-right through a final field, before Limington, to reach a stile beside a signpost giving access to a road. Go right along this road for 18 metres (20 yards).

8. Turn left to follow a signposted footpath, cross a stile to enter a field and aim for a squeeze stile at the right-hand end of iron railings ahead. Bear right towards St Mary's Church, Limington. Go left to join the road and turn right to follow it through the village, soon taking a bend on your left. Turn right over a stile beside a waymarked gate. Walk with a wall on your right, follow the Monarch's Way through a gate in the corner ahead and continue to the far right-hand corner of the next field where a stile gives access to a small footbridge on your right. Cross this and bear left to cross a much bigger footbridge and rejoin your outward route. Go left, soon taking a small, wooden, waymarked gate, to retrace your steps to Ilchester. This route is shared by the waymarked Leland Trail and the waymarked Monarch's Way. The Leland Trail runs for 28 miles from Alfred's Tower to Ham Hill, all within Somerset.

26. Cadbury Castle

Route: St Thomas à Becket's Church, South Cadbury – King Arthur's Well, Cadbury Castle – Queen Anne's Wishing Well, Cadbury Castle – Arthur's Palace, Cadbury Castle – St Thomas à Becket's Church, South Cadbury

Distance: 2 miles. Moderate.

Maps: O.S. Explorer 129 Yeovil & Sherborne; O.S. Landranger 183 Yeovil & Frome.

Start: St Thomas à Becket's Church, South Cadbury (ST 632255)

Access: An infrequent bus (no 19 or 19A) runs to South Cadbury from Bruton. Buses nos. 1 (Yeovil-Shepton Mallet) and 2 (Yeovil-Bruton) run more frequently to North Cadbury, which is two miles north of South Cadbury. Tel. 01823 – 358299 for details.

Round and About

King Arthur's Camelot?

This is the place to maintain a midnight vigil if you wish to glimpse the legendary King Arthur as the leader of the Wild Hunt. Or rather not, instead to bury your head in the ground and hope you will not be seen and carried off to the Celtic Underworld. The lack of survivors from such a risky venture means that nobody is quite sure when to come. Is it on the eve of the summer solstice, the winter solstice, Christmas, the nearest full moon, Samhain, Imbolc, corresponding dates in the old calendar (add 11 days), every year, every seven years or 19? Anyway, come equipped with your protecting rowan twigs and sprigs of heather and watch out! It may be that you will just see Arthur and his knights. They are said to ride out from Cadbury castle and water their horses at the spring near the church at Sutton Montis, just to the south of here. The more sinister Wild Hunt is usually associated with a line running north-north-west towards Glastonbury Tor from Queen Anne's Wishing Well. This is at an angle of 320 degrees, marking the moonset at the northerly major lunar standstill (and, in the other direction, moonrise in the southerly major standstill). There is a clear view of Glastonbury Tor from Cadbury Castle. The distance is some 11 miles and experiments have proved how beacons could be seen from each place, so they could have formed part of a signalling system of beacon hills.

Cadbury Castle

Burrowbridge Mump

Another major line, ley or spirit path comes at an angle of 63 degrees from the northern edge of Hamdon Hill in the west-southwest, again over a distance of some 11 miles. This angle marks the Beltane (early May) and Lughnasadh (early August) sunrises (and, in the other direction, sunsets at Samhain in early November and Imbolc in early February). Cadbury Castle forms the eastern point of a parallelogram or rhombus whose western point is at Burrowbridge Mump.

Now partly obscured by trees, this Iron Age hillfort has four lines of bank and ditch defences. Excavations in the late 1960s revealed a foundation sacrifice as well as evidence that the Romans finally managed to capture this place around AD 70, which was rather late. Did the famous King Arviragus hold out here and is he the Arthur whose ghost is seen? This may not have been the southern outpost of his Silurian kingdom. The Durotriges tribe (from Dorset) may have been its occupants. Anyway, the Romans cleared them out for three or four hundred years. Then, rather interestingly, Cadbury Castle was re-occupied in the late fifth century and a great feasting hall was erected on the site known by locals for centuries as being where Arthur's Palace is believed to have stood.

It was John Leland who reported, in 1542, that 'at the very south ende of the churche of South-Cadbyri standith Camallate, sumtyme a famous toun or castelle', and 'the people can tell nothing ther but that they have hard say that Arture much resortid to Camalat.' So, was Cadbury Castle the famous King Arthur's Camelot? It certainly occupied a strategic position. Given that the possibly-mythical sixth-century Arthur of *The Mabinogion* and *The Lives of the British Saints* was allegedly based in Gwent, this would be a major fort guarding his southern frontier (with Cerdic?) rather than a central capital. There may have been a fifth-century Arthur, remembering that the Arth Fawr (Great Bear) could have been a title as well as a name, active in the south-west of what became England.

The best-known sixth-century Arthur is known to have ruled this part of Somerset jointly with Cadwy, the son of Geraint. Cadbury could mean Cadwy's settlement. As for Camelot, that could be derived from Camulos, a Celtic god of war. An excellent forum for Arthurian debate is *Pendragon*, the magazine of the Pendragon Society, c/o John and Linda Ford, 41 Ridge Street, Watford, Herts, WD2 5BL.

You can also see the wall-painting of St Thomas à Becket in the church dedicated to him, and where this walk begins.

The Walk

1. Face St Thomas à Becket's Church and go left. Turn right up Castle Lane. This is the access track to Cadbury Castle.

2. Half-way up, through the hill-fort's earthworks, take a path on your left which immediately passes a well on your right which is known as King Arthur's Well. Walk around the hill-fort, soon emerging into a cleared section of the earthwork, facing south. Keep below the top bank.

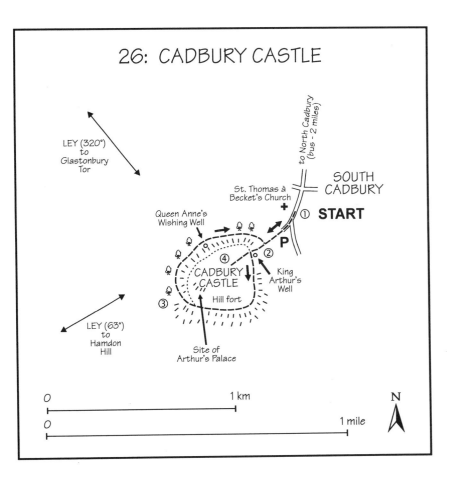

3. Fork left along the lower path which goes through the woodland and leads to a muddy patch on your right where a stone trough marks Queen Anne's Wishing Well. Continue until you are back on the access lane. Turn right to climb up into the vast central plateau of the hill-fort. Climb to the site of Arthur's Palace in the highest, far-right (south-western) corner.

4. Retrace your steps from Cadbury Castle, along Castle Lane and left to return to St Thomas à Becket's Church, South Cadbury.

27. Broadway

Route: Broadway – Church-Stovard Coppice-Broadway

Distance: 2¼ miles. Easy.

Maps: O.S. Explorer 128 Taunton and Blackdown Hills; O.S. Landranger 193 Taunton and Lyme Regis.

Start: Broadway war memorial (ST320154).

Access: Bus no. 31 (or 31C but *not* X31) runs to Broadway from Taunton and Weymouth, tel. 01823 358299.

Round and About

Black Shuck

Broadway's parish church is dedicated to the seventh-century Saxon St Aldhelm and to St Eadburgha, probably the daughter of Centwine, a seventh-century King of Wessex and descendant of the Briton Cerdic, leader of the Gewissae. This suggests an ancient sacred site which may be on a ley running due west (in line with sunset at the equinoxes) to Castle Neroche at ST271158. The church stands isolated from the village today, but E.W. Ryall, author of *Second Time Round*, remembers it during a previous incarnation when he was John Fletcher.

John's first love was the beautiful Melanie, a lady of independent spirit who 'was above medium height, with long ringlet curls as dark as midnight, bewitching brown eyes and rosy cheeks'. She belonged to one of the best families in Somerset, the Pouletts of Hinton St George, with the blood of the Norman de Warenne in her veins. Writing about how Melanie and John rode the leafy lane towards Broadway and of his eventual return to this village in this life, E.W. Ryall was surprised to see the village so far apart from the 1655 church. The two lovers rode there in March, 1665. That year the Great Plague affected the village, and the old buildings were deserted, leading the population to move westwards from the church. As Melanie and John approached the church, they were overtaken by a 'great black hound' which drew ahead 'powerfully, but soundlessly'. Their horses 'showed signs of great agitation, needing much urging to follow after the surly beast'. The beast 'turned its head towards us and bestowed upon us a most malevolent glare, with its large, yellow eyes as luminous as a dozen best wax candles. Then it bounded the church wall, hard by the ladies' mounting-stones, and ran towards the tower'. The lovers knew they had seen Black Shuck, signifying the death of one or both of them within a year. Melanie died of the Great Plague later in 1665. There doesn't seem to be a mounting-block at the church now, but has it been moved to outside the village stores? There are still sightings of a 'black beast' in the neighbourhood.

The Walk

1. Face the war memorial, turn left along Broadway Road and pass Goose Lane and the village stores on your right. Pass restored 17th century almshouses on your left (known to the lovers John and Melanie in 1665). Pass Sugg's Lane on your right and continue to the church dedicated to St Aldhelm and St Eadburgha on your right.

2. Turn left through a gate across the road from the church to take the signposted public footpath towards Ashill. Walk beside a hedge on your left, go through a gap in the hedge ahead and continue across a narrow field. Take a gap in the hedge ahead and walk near the hedge on your right in the next field. Go through another gap in its far right-hand corner ahead to continue with a hedge on your right in this fourth field.

3. Do not take the footbridge and wooden gate in the corner ahead. Turn left to walk with the ditch and hedge on your right. Continue through a gap into the next field, still with the

hedge on your right. Go ahead over a wooden stile to enter a third field. Bear half-right through this, ignoring two gates in the hedge away to your right. Take a gate in its far right corner ahead. Bear half-left to reach a stile half-way along the hedge running along the left-hand side of this field.

4. Turn left to cross the stile and take a path ahead into Stovard Coppice. Walk just inside this, with its perimeter hedge on your left and woodland on your right. Emerge from the coppice to maintain your direction, keeping beside a hedge on your left. Take a gate and bear right along a firm track.

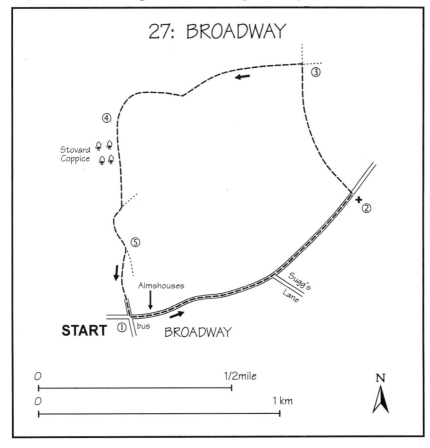

5. Reach a corner of grass on your right and fork right off the firm
track here to take a narrow passage in the hedge ahead, cross a
footbridge and a subsequent stile. Walk along the left-hand
side of a field. Cross a stile at its far end to walk between
houses and return to the war memorial, village stores and bus
stop in the centre of modern Broadway.

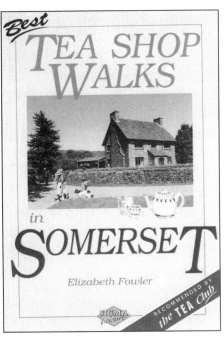

Also of Interest:

BEST TEA SHOP WALKS IN SOMERSET

Elizabeth Fowler

These walks are all circular, from 2 to 9 miles and are accompanied by explanatory text on the half hidden pearls of interest to be found along the way. To complete the experience you are invited to visit the tea rooms in the towns and villages featured on the routes, each an excellent quality (and well-deserved!) refreshment break. *£6.95*

WALKS IN MYSTERIOUS WILTSHIRE

Laurence Main

Step into secret Wiltshire, one of the most mysterious of English counties, containing Stonehenge, Avebury, several white horses and now seasonally visited by crop circles! 27 routes, suitable for all ages and abilities, take you into enchanting walking countryside, and a world of discovery. *£6.95*

WALKS IN MYSTERIOUS OXFORDSHIRE

Laurence Main

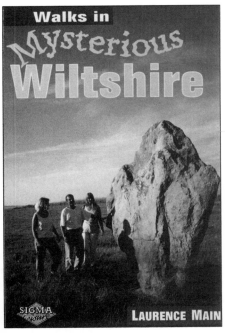

Follow the leylines that connect holy hills and sacred sites, search for a lost giant, explore the river dedicated the goddess Isis and follow the spirit path to Banbury Cross, where the white horse overlooks Uffington. "...an attractively presented book which makes you want to pull your boots on and start exploring" BOOTPRINT. *£6.95*